UNSHAKABLE

I've attended Times Square Church for many years and never fail to hear the pure and anointed Word of God from its godly pastors. It's a great joy and a deep comfort to know that God's voice is speaking "for such a time as this" in New York City and beyond.

Eric Metaxas
New York Times Bestselling Author of *Bonhoeffer: Pastor, Martyr, Prophet, Spy*

This generation has grown weary of the commentators and pundits who stammer through attempts to explain what's going on in our society. How wonderfully refreshing it is to have a pastor unapologetically not only give definition to our current situation but also, with spiritual discernment, give us insight as to what we are to expect in the future. *Unshakable* is a prophetic word that every believer should not only read but heed.

Lamar Vest
Former President and CEO of the American Bible Society

As a generation clings desperately to their worldly possessions in the face of looming poverty, Carter Conlon preaches an unshakable gospel of Christ crucified and confidence found only in the cross.

John Hoover
New York Times Bestselling Author

I've had the wonderful opportunity to visit Times Square Church on Sundays when I have been in New York. I learned quickly to get there very early, as seats are packed an hour before the service. Once hearing Pastor Carter Conlon, it's easy to understand why. The church defies all explanation. Located right in the very heart of New York's Times Square/Theater District, it attracts people of all faiths, races, ethnic groups and backgrounds. They experience some of the most powerful praise and worship on earth and solid, biblical preaching from Pastor Conlon. I've been blessed every time I've been there. I hope you will be as encouraged by Pastor Conlon's new book and that it will speak to you as if you're sitting in the congregation at Times Square Church.

Mike Huckabee
Governor of Arkansas
Host of "Huckabee" (FOX News) and *New York Times* Bestselling Author of *A Simple Government: Twelve Things We Really Need from Government*

This work is timely and of benefit to any Christian who wants to walk the biblical way. I have known Pastor Conlon for many years, and he lives this life as well as the church he shepherds. His life and devotion to God attest to the fact that the subject matter he's dealing with is relevant for our times. I highly recommend this great work.

L. John Bueno
Executive Director (Retired) of Assemblies of God World Missions

I have had the opportunity to hear Pastor Carter Conlon speak, and each time I was impressed at how he was always able to bring the message home to the people. He was discipled by my dear friend and spiritual father, David Wilkerson. I am so thankful for the legacy of strong Bible-based preaching and ministry that Pastor Carter brings to Times Square Church.

Nicky Cruz
Nicky Cruz Outreach

Pastor Carter Conlon is a true man of God who lives what he preaches. He has been given a special anointing of the Holy Spirit to deliver the Word of God with straightforwardness and authority, yet with mercy and grace. When this man preaches, you know you have truly heard from God's throne.

David Wilkerson (1931–2011)
Founding Pastor, Times Square Church, New York

In these uncertain times, we need to have a hope and confidence that will see us through. *Unshakable* shares the amazing insights from God's Word that we can not only survive difficult and perilous times but actually grow in faith, confidence and boldness through them. God is not looking for a fearful people who whimper into their futures but those who know His heart and are as bold as lions. This book will serve as a roadmap to that boldness.

Gary Wilkerson
President, World Challenge
Founding Pastor, The Springs Church, Colorado Springs, Colorado

CARTER CONLON

UNSHAKABLE

TRUSTING **GOD**
WHEN ALL ELSE FAILS

Regal

For more information and
special offers from Regal Books, email us at
subscribe@regalbooks.com

Published by Regal
From Gospel Light
Ventura, California, U.S.A.
www.regalbooks.com
Printed in the U.S.A.

Library of Congress Cataloging-in-Publication Data
Conlon, Carter.
Unshakable : trusting God when all else fails / Carter Conlon.
pages cm
Includes bibliographical references and index.
ISBN 978-0-8307-6541-6 (alk. paper)
1. Trust in God—Christianity. I. Title.
BV4637.C583 2013
248.4—dc23
2013001399

Rights for publishing this book outside the U.S.A. or in non-English
languages are administered by Gospel Light Worldwide, an international
not-for-profit ministry. For additional information, please visit
www.glww.org, email info@glww.org, or write to Gospel Light Worldwide,
1957 Eastman Avenue, Ventura, CA 93003, U.S.A.

To order copies of this book and other Regal products in bulk quantities,
please contact us at 1-800-446-7735.

To Jason, Jared and Katie.
With much love, Dad.

CONTENTS

Acknowledgments 11

Foreword (Pastor Claude Houde) 13

Preface 19

Part 1: Understanding the Season

1. Appraisal Time..23

2. Days of Difficulty: Behind the Scenes 37

Part 2: Divine Deposits

3. More Precious than Gold..............................61

4. Some Things Cannot Be Learned from a Book.........75

5. A Right Response...93

Part 3: Unlocking an Endless Supply

6. Where Shall I Invest? 113

7. The Key to the Storehouse............................133

8. The Last Bank in America............................155

ACKNOWLEDGMENTS

To Leslie Quon, Tammy Shannon and so many of the Times Square Church staff who have dedicated their lives and sacrificially given of their time and talent to get the incredible message of the gospel to so many who need to hear it. Thank you.

FOREWORD

I have known Pastor Carter Conlon for more than 25 years. I remember so vividly the first time we met. As a Montreal pastor and president of a Christian association reaching to the French world, I was invited to participate in a special event that gathered Christian leaders from all over Canada to pray for our country. The all-day event, held on the steps of our nation's Parliament building, brought together thousands of believers and the most well-known Canadian pastors, evangelists and Christian leaders of national ministries, Bible colleges and humanitarian agencies, who took turns on stage to speak and pray. The event was extremely well organized. Christian bands played great music and powerful multimedia presentations were offered.

However, the crowd was loud and unruly. Thousands were coming and going and, at some points in the day, it seemed as if the speakers were going almost entirely unnoticed in the midst of the noise of the crowd. I was standing away from the stage, giving an interview to a national media, when a man began to pray at the microphone. I didn't catch his name. He made no opening remarks, had no witty icebreakers, had no axe to grind, did not promote his ministry, and did not enumerate his pedigree or accomplishments. He just prayed.

Now, please understand that during my 30 years of ministry I have been privileged to minister in more than 35 countries, and I have ministered in thousands of services in the most diverse settings. I have prayed and heard people pray pretty much every day of my life for more than three decades. But as this man of God began to pray for our nation, a hush came over the boisterous crowd. I had never seen anything like it. Silence, reverence and prayer filled the field. The journalists stopped asking questions, families joined hands, spontaneous small groups formed to intercede together, people wept openly, police officers bowed their heads, and thousands began to pray. His crying out to God was fervent, humble, anointed, and filled with compassion and love—a passionate call to Christ filled with hope.

"Who is this man?" I asked the organizers of the event. "That's Pastor Carter Conlon," they replied.

Over the years, as I reflected on that divine moment, I have come to a clear understanding of what impressed me most about the man who prayed that day: it was his faith. It was and *is* unshakable. I believe Pastor Carter has been raised by the hand of the Lord with a message from heaven for such a time as this.

As a bilingual pastor able to translate from English to French, I have been privileged to stand by some of the most influential ministries of our era and see "behind the scenes" who these men and women were away from the spotlight and stage. I have seen up close Pastor Carter's faith through trials, battle with sickness, immense pressures and valleys of grief. I have seen him confront fierce spiritual opposition and what seemed to me insurmountable mountains of impossibilities as he ministered to tens of thousands in post-genocide African nations or in the most evil and crime-infested places on earth. *Unshakable* is more than a series of messages on a fascinating topic. It is the life, testimonies, miracle stories and principles of faith born and tested through the fire of a man who lives and imparts faith—a man who calls to resurrection what was dead, sees the invisible, and births the miraculous. Page by page, you will be strengthened, convicted and challenged. I am convinced you will receive fresh life, your heart will burn, and you will find an anchor for your soul.

Out of the abundance of the heart the mouth speaks (and the pen writes!). Pastor Carter's faith is unshakable.

Carter Conlon

That's his heart as a man of God speaking and writing to millions and as a husband, father, grandfather and mentor to countless believers and servants of the Lord around the world. These pages come from a lifetime of serving and trusting God, and they will ignite your spirit, resurrect your confidence in God's promises, and equip you for the times you are called to live in. The truths you will discover in this book are eternal, but they are God's word for His Church in the twenty-first century. They are God's message for His people today. As everything that can be shaken will be, God is raising up a people who will learn to trust in Him when all else fails.

Pastor Carter shows us the way.

Pastor Claude Houde
Montreal, February 2013

UNSHAKABLE

PREFACE

You hold this book in your hands. You have believed and trusted in God. You started out with much faith and promise for the future, but now you often feel like the psalmist who cried, "My God, my God, why have You forsaken me? Why don't You help me and answer my cries?" (see Ps. 22:1). You wonder if there could possibly be any good purpose to what you have been and may be going through.

What if I told you there *is* a divine purpose? Would you be surprised to learn that you are in the very center of God's will for your life?

We are entering a perilous time in history in which your life and testimony will be priceless currency for the kingdom of God. Jesus is putting a deposit of His life within you for the sake of others. He is making you unshakable. Many people will soon come to you, asking you for the reason you have such hope when so many are losing theirs. They will be looking to draw from your strength. You are the "last bank in America."

Please read the following pages carefully to understand how and why this is true. The truth will set you free, and the hope of many others will soon depend on it!

Carter Conlon

PART 1

UNDERSTANDING
THE SEASON

1

APPRAISAL TIME

*Let us search and try our ways, and turn
again to the LORD.*

LAMENTATIONS 3:40

UNSHAKABLE

A mere glance at today's headlines shows us that we are all on the same page: it is no longer debatable that we have reached a crisis point in history. Not only are multiple nations dealing with political, economic and social confusion within their own borders, we are also living in a volatile season in which everything could radically change on a global scale in a moment of time—particularly as we stand on the brink of a worldwide economic collapse.

Crisis moments require us to be courageous enough to deal with the issues of our day and, more importantly, those that lie within our own hearts. It is time for an appraisal. Not of our assets, not of our property. We need to probe deeper. It is time for us to stop and seriously consider where we are headed as a nation. Are you and I prepared for what is coming? Do we have resident within us what we need to face the coming days?

In North America today, I fear that even many Christians are largely unaware of the depth of the great trial rapidly coming upon us and, sadly, possess little inner resource to meet it. We profess our devotion to Christ without much difficulty when the sun is out, the paycheck is in the mailbox, and there is still food on the table. Yet it is when we strike the iceberg that, in the same manner as the RMS *Titanic,* suddenly our hearts and motives will be unveiled. That is when it will become evident if our security is truly rooted in Christ alone. We will discover whether or not our hearts will prove to be steadfast, with the express purpose of living for the glory of God and the souls of men.

If we expect to be found unshakable in the days to come, I can only arrive at this one conclusion: an immediate and deliberate decision must be made in our hearts to go the full journey with Christ. We do not have a lot of time to get this right. It is now that we face the critical choice: are we in, or are we out?

Bear in mind that following Christ for the full journey, in the manner that God has prescribed in His Word, was never promised to be an easy path. Yet I daresay that the half-hearted simply will not make it. In fact, the Scriptures warn us that a whole contingency who claim to be part of the kingdom of God will soon realize that they have no life, no power, no spiritual vision (see Matt. 25:8). They will find themselves seized with panic during the hour of crisis.

This is precisely why it is imperative that we take the time to search our hearts now. If you have not yet made the choice, or you have somehow grown discouraged along the way, my prayer is that by the end of this book you will be fully persuaded to follow Christ wholeheartedly.

Of course, this is no light undertaking that can simply be settled with an ardent declaration, "I will follow You, Lord, even unto death." The disciples once made such a vehement boast, only to end up deserting Christ in the hour of crisis. Such a decision ought to be made with at least a measure of discernment of the times in which we live, as well as an understanding of what it really means to walk with Christ.

Contrary to modern-day theology, God never promised us a life without trials and suffering, but rather one in which we would be refined and carefully molded into His image. He never intended for us to settle for the narrow life of living solely for ourselves with affections set on the things of this world, but rather to live with hands outstretched and hearts touched by the infirmities of others.

A willing embracing of such truths, which we will further examine in the coming chapters, will no doubt be met with a sovereign strengthening from the Lord. He will strengthen us so that our hearts will not fail—not only in the coming difficult days but also now as we undergo God's process for preparing a people fit to dispense His provision to a world in dire need.

So let us begin by considering how we as a nation, and much of the Western world, ended up here in the first place. I believe it will help put things into perspective and prepare us for where we are headed in the days to come.

UNHEEDED WARNINGS

It has become evident over the course of history that the ways of humanity do not change. Therefore, it is often easy for us to see ourselves in the mirror of God's Word. Consider, for example, Paul's journey in Acts 27. I believe it paints a remarkably clear picture of where we have come from and where we are going as a society today.

Paul was a prisoner at the time, on a ship headed for Italy where he was to testify before Caesar. Having made a landing in Crete, Paul knew that to continue sailing on this journey meant that they were all headed for peril. The captain and crew of the ship, however, were unaware of the danger ahead—just as much of our generation has been oblivious to the fact that continuing on this pathway of our own choosing will eventually take us into a storm of unprecedented proportions.

> Now when much time was spent, and when sailing was now dangerous, because the fast was now already past, Paul admonished them, and

said unto them, Sirs, I perceive that this voyage will be with hurt and much damage, not only of the lading and ship, but also of our lives. Nevertheless the centurion believed the master and the owner of the ship, more than those things which were spoken by Paul (Acts 27:9-11).

Paul's simple warning to the men was completely disregarded. He was a type of the Word of God sent to a self-willed, stubborn generation.

The majority advised to set sail from there. . . . When the south wind blew softly, supposing that they had obtained their desire, putting out to sea, they sailed close by Crete (vv. 12-13, *NKJV*).

Have we as a society not done the very same thing—disregarding the Lord's faithful warnings for us to turn from our own ways, to turn from the arrogance of believing that we have the right and the wisdom to chart our own course? Off we sailed in our selfish pursuits, trying to grasp something of this world that would allow us to be our own god and to determine our own destiny, something that would allow us to defy the lordship of Jesus Christ and still reach what we consider to be some utopian end. At first the soft wind blows, and we believe it portends a favorable voyage ahead. Surely we are on our way to prosperity, fame and good days! If only we had eyes to see what really lies ahead.

PROPHECY FULFILLED

Don't think that God did not issue numerous warnings to our generation before we embarked on this journey far away from His heart. He has warned us not only through examples in the Scriptures but also through many voices that have been raised in our society—servants of God with the ability to discern the times. David Wilkerson was such a one.

A vision was given to him in the early 1970s, and it was published in 1973 in a book entitled *The Vision*. In a season of seeking God in prayer, the Lord began to unlock before Pastor David a glimpse of what was to come—the future of America, the future of societies around the world. He grappled deeply with publishing this vision, for he was aware that it would bring him reproach among people in the Christian community who would refuse to hear such things. No man or woman willingly wants to go to a place where they will be mocked or thought of as off base. But Pastor David weighed carefully what God had given him, and he put it into print. Consider the following excerpt from *The Vision*, bearing in mind the year it was written:

There is worldwide economic confusion just ahead. In my vision, this is the clearest thing I have seen. Many praying people now share this very same vision.

Not only is the American dollar headed for deep trouble, but so are all other world currencies. I see total economic confusion striking Europe first and then affecting Japan, the United States, Canada, and all other nations shortly thereafter.

It is not really a depression I see coming— but a recession of such magnitude that it will affect the lifestyle of nearly every wage earner in America and around the world. Countries that now control huge amounts of Western currency are going to be in very deep trouble also. Arab countries will especially be hurt.

Without a doubt, there are lean years ahead full of monetary confusion and despair. How soon is not clear, but it is not far away. The world's economists will be at a loss to explain the confusion, and an international crisis of fear will develop. A false economic boom will precede the recession—but it will be short-lived.

In spite of all the danger signs around us warning of impending economic disaster, the next few years (from 1973) will be among the most prosperous in the history of mankind. They will be fat and flourishing years. In spite of tight money policies, people will continue to spend freely. Sales will continue to break records and people will spend more than ever in modern history. Credit debt will become nearly uncontrollable.

I see, very clearly, just a few years of tremendous affluence and continued economic prosperity. Church budgets will increase, wages will increase—missionary giving will also increase.

Inflation, costs, and wages will spiral higher and higher. . . .

I believe we are going to witness the bankruptcies of some of this nation's major and most popular corporations. I see tremendous difficulty arising for credit corporations. There are going to be many people unable to pay off their heavy obligations to major credit card companies, causing near-chaos.

Thousands of small businesses will also be forced into bankruptcies. . . .

The United States government is going to "overreact" to the confused economical developments.

I see a flurry of near-panic decisions being made by various government agencies—but these hasty efforts to shore up the economy will backfire.

Amazing, isn't it? You would think you were reading today's *New York Times*.

David Wilkerson did end up paying a price for his message. For almost forty years he was a lone voice in the Western world, when everything seemed to be moving in the opposite direction of what he had proclaimed. Some people may have given a passing thought to the warnings, but in many cases they were not taken seriously. Instead, the majority of society moved toward the very things that Pastor David often warned would result in an onset of spiritual blindness.

Over and over we see this in the Scriptures. The one voice that a society in spiritual decline will not listen to is the voice of warning. Think of Noah, who was called a preacher of righteousness in his generation. For more than a hundred years, he prepared an ark while constantly warning the people of an impending flood. Most likely some people actually believed him. Yet day after day as they passed by Noah, they began to conclude in their hearts, "No, a great flood cannot come. The Lord would not send a flood just yet. I'm really starting to enjoy this good life. I have a great vision for myself that has yet to be fulfilled. I finally started my business and just got a huge farm that is very dear to me. Surely the Lord would not give me all these things and then suddenly come and take me away to heaven!" Others might have passed by saying, "Oh, don't listen to Noah, he is too extreme. We do believe there is a coming day of judgment, but it is not as close as he says it is." And so they grew complacent with the warnings of God.

What happened to the other prophets of old whom God sent to warn His people? In short, they were mocked, threatened, cast into prison, thrown into pits, starved, stoned and killed. King Jehoiakim brazenly cut up a scroll with the words of the prophet Jeremiah, throwing it section by section into the fire until the whole thing was consumed (see Jer. 36:22-23).

Even the people in Isaiah's day refused to listen to the warnings that the Lord sent through His prophet. Notice the reason for their hardness of heart: "Their land also is full of silver and gold, neither is there any end of their treasures; their land is also full of horses, neither is there any end of their chariots" (Isa. 2:7). They looked around and said, "Listen, we have silver, we have gold, we have treasures, not to mention the mightiest army in the world. What do you mean that it is all going to come down? What do you mean that hardship is ahead of us, since we are clearly at the zenith of prosperity? We already have a plan to get out of every situation that we might find ourselves in. We have formed political alliances that will guarantee us security in the future. Are you blind, Isaiah? Don't you see what we have?"

Momentary prosperity had blinded them. In the same way, this attitude has been the general sentiment over the past few decades, particularly in the Western world. To this day, there are people who try to remain optimistic, convincing themselves that we are not headed into an economic tailspin. However, those who are willing to face reality are beginning to see that there *is* an end to our silver, gold and treasures in sight.

It is now the fortieth year since this warning was published in *The Vision*. Aside from the fact that there is clear spiritual significance in the 40-day and 40-year periods found throughout the Bible, there is something else that I see time and again in the Scriptures: the Lord will send His warning and allow a season for us to consider our ways—a season during which we might think about how we are living, what we are investing in, where our hope lies and how prepared we are to face the coming days.

And so today we stand at a critical junction. The question is, will we heed the Lord's warnings? Will we take seriously this window of time we have been given to search our hearts? I can only echo the plea of the prophet Jeremiah: "Let us search and try our ways, and turn again to the LORD" (Lam. 3:40).

2

DAYS OF DIFFICULTY: BEHIND THE SCENES

Indeed, the Sovereign LORD never does anything until he reveals his plans to his servants the prophets.

AMOS 3:7, *NLT*

UN SHAKABLE

The Scriptures tell us that the children of Israel knew God's acts, but Moses understood His ways (see Ps. 103:7). If ever there was a time to understand the ways of God, it is now. The enemy will no doubt use the intensifying global upheaval to further his agenda in masking the goodness of God from the eyes of many. Yet if you and I are able to catch a glimpse of what God is doing behind the scenes—both on a societal as well as a personal level—it will help us not to lose heart in the coming days. That is why it is critical that we understand His ways now, recognizing that we are living in an hour of great mercy.

Before we consider things on a more personal level, make no mistake about our destination as a society: you and I are headed for the wilderness. In light of the turmoil we are already facing in this nation, I realize that this is the last thing many people want to hear right now. Nevertheless, I cannot disregard what the Holy Spirit has been impressing on my heart for years.

What do I mean when I speak of the wilderness? First of all, the wilderness is a place of dryness, famine and incredible hardship; a place where familiar comforts are stripped away. Yet more importantly, the wilderness is a place that brings us to a total dependence on God. All of society, including the whole Church, is going to meet there, and it is going to happen very soon. I don't know exactly how hard it is going to be; I just feel that it is going to be extremely difficult for everybody. Events around us bear witness to this sentiment almost every day.

Over the years, we pastors at Times Square Church have not held back from warning our congregation of the perilous days ahead. The risk in that, I suppose, is that some people may feel they have heard the warning for so long that eventually it just becomes part of the mantra to them. After a while their ears grow dull to the message—almost the same way we tend to ignore the safety demonstration before the plane takes off. However, there *is* a time when a plane goes down.

Then there are other people who have such an aversion to the idea of hardship that they immediately shut down at the mere mention of the word "wilderness." If they don't hear a message that makes them happy and assures them that everything is going to be fine, they quickly leave in search of a place where they will hear some good news. Yet what this displays is an inherent lack of understanding of the ways of God. People ultimately do themselves a great disservice when they pursue God in this way, for in reality, this *is* good news. At the core of it all is the mercy of God.

If you will open your heart and allow the Holy Spirit to speak to you, you will find great peace and strength in this word. In the days ahead, when others are running around confused and terrified, you will not be shaken. You will discover that the Lord has already prepared you.

Time after time at our church, we have seen God's faithfulness to lead and prepare us for things to come. For example, in September of 2012, we launched *Feed New York*, an initiative to help start and support feeding programs throughout the greater New York City area. Our initial commitment was to partner with 100 churches and underwrite their feeding programs for a year. As the applications came in, it was exciting to find that so many churches of various denominations shared this vision of feeding the hungry in our city. We could not help but sense that something significant was underway. The Lord was breaking down barriers and bringing unity among His people once again.

The first food delivery to one of our partner churches was made on October 23, 2012. Six days later, Hurricane Sandy hit—ravaging regions throughout the eastern seaboard and leaving areas of New York and New Jersey decimated.

When something this momentous occurs, those who have been listening to the Lord's message all along should not be caught off guard. They should instinctively know that God has been preparing them for these very moments—which, in fact, became evident in this case. Within days of the storm's onset, hundreds of volunteers showed up at our church ready to bag groceries, sort donations or be dispatched to help with relief efforts in some of the most devastated areas. There was divine order as God's people were mobilized to reach out to a city in need. I even saw people who had suffered significant losses of their own helping out where they could. In spite of their personal hardship, they were joining teams to help gut homes and offer comfort to others in despair.

On top of all this, we began to realize, at least in part, why the Holy Spirit had impressed it upon on our hearts to start *Feed New York*. Because of our launch of this initiative the month before, relationships with churches throughout the different boroughs were already being established. After the storm hit, we had food, water and supplies quickly delivered to a number of our partner churches, who were in turn prepared to distribute the supplies within their own communities. This marks what I believe is only the beginning of what the Lord intends to do as His Church walks in unity.

As we witnessed, God is always faithful to strengthen and strategically prepare His people for whatever they will have to face. However, this means that we must be careful to incline our ears to what He is speaking, particularly regarding things to come. The people who are constantly searching for a more palatable message will ultimately be excluded from partaking of God's strength in the days ahead. The Lord imparts this divine strength to believers who are not afraid to listen to what the Holy Spirit is speaking and are therefore able to discern the times. It is in this context that I urge you to open your heart—to recognize the hour in which we live and to begin to understand that the Lord is issuing a great mercy call.

THE END OF HUMAN SCHEMES

Paul and those with him on the ship were headed for disaster due to foolish decisions. In the same way, despite all God's warnings, we as a society have chosen over the past several decades to embark on a journey far away from God's heart—a journey toward self-destruction. It is no surprise, therefore, that our generation is beginning to find itself at a point of desperation, similar to the despair of Paul's companions shortly after they set sail.

But not long after there arose against it a tempestuous wind, called Euroclydon. And when the ship was caught, and could not bear up into the wind, we let her drive. And running under a certain island which is called Clauda, we had much work to come by the boat: which when they had taken up, they used helps, undergirding the ship; and, fearing lest they should fall into the quicksands, strake sail, and so were driven. And we being exceedingly tossed with a tempest, the next day they lightened the ship; and the third day we cast out with our own hands the tackling of the ship (Acts 27:14-19).

A storm arose—a storm such as they had never experienced. Everyone on that ship was perplexed. As gale-force winds battered them, the crew lowered the anchor and struggled to strengthen and secure the ship. Finally, when they had exhausted all their ideas and "helps," they began throwing everything overboard.

What a parallel to our day! All of a sudden, we find ourselves in the midst of a series of storms so confounding that nobody knows how to handle things anymore. Not only did we recently experience Hurricane Sandy, a physical storm, here in the Northeast, but we are witnessing the constant crumbling of the very infrastructure of this country—the breakdown of the family, the redefining of marriage, the collapse of our financial system, the ineptitude of our political system. All the while, due to society's determination to eradicate everything that has to do with the name of Christ and the value system of God, the whole country is on a moral landslide that ought to terrify every man's heart.

It seems that everything is falling apart at the same time. We tried our best to tie the ship together and keep advancing in the midst of the storm. We employed every strategy we could conjure up in attempts to save a tanking economy, yet all of our collective efforts have proven futile. Has it finally dawned on us that in all of our planning and scheming, we are merely rearranging chairs on the deck of the Titanic?

In His great mercy, God is now speaking to a generation that for so long has been seeking security and fulfillment in the things of this world—a generation of people who thought that money, fame and power would satisfy the deepest desires of their hearts. We arrogantly believed that our own wisdom would see us through, yet all it has led to is a storm. Now pride is starting to die, and reality is setting in, for God has mercifully allowed society to reach a point where we will have no other choice but to cast all our human effort overboard.

THE RETURN OF HIS BRIDE

Not only will God allow the storm to put an end to wrong pursuits and human schemes, I believe He is also after something much deeper. At the core of it all, we will find God's jealousy over His Bride—His Church—and His yearning for her return to Him.

Jesus once cried over His own people, "O Jerusalem, Jerusalem, . . . how often would I have gathered thy children together, even as a hen gathereth her chickens under her wings" (Matt. 23:37). Jesus referred to the inhabitants of the city of Jerusalem as if they were one person, like a bride who had been brought into a place of worthiness so that she might honor Him. Yet somehow this bride had fallen drastically from her calling in the earth.

We can hear the underlying longing in the Lord's cry, much like a brokenhearted bridegroom who comes home to discover that his bride has not been faithful: "How I wanted you as My bride! I wanted you as My very own. I wanted to draw you into the closeness of My heart so that the two of us would walk together as one." The Lord is aware that something has captivated the heart of His Bride, and He is determined to get it back—even if it means that He must draw her into the wilderness.

In the book of Hosea, we see this pattern of how God deals with His own people when they have strayed from His truth and purposes for them:

> For their mother hath played the harlot: she that conceived them hath done shamefully: for she said, I will go after my lovers, that give me my bread and my water, my wool and my flax, mine oil and my drink (Hos. 2:5).

The Lord intended for His own people to be a praise on the earth. Yet somewhere along the way, His Bride became so enamored with the things of this world that she lost her heart for the actual work of God. Rather than embracing the true gospel, her heart became inextricably attached to this world. She was diverted from her husband and began to seek material things.

> Therefore, behold, I will hedge up thy way with thorns, and make a wall, that she shall not find her paths. And she shall follow after her lovers, but she shall not overtake them; and she shall seek them, but shall not find them: then shall she say, I will go and return to my first husband; for then was it better with me than now (vv. 6-7).

In other words, the Lord said, "I am going to stop this procession. She will be searching for things that she has been trusting in for security and pleasure, but she will not find them. I am going to stop this pathway and turn her around."

> For she did not know that I gave her corn, and wine, and oil, and multiplied her silver and gold, which they prepared for Baal (v. 8).

Baal was a Canaanite god—the god of provision. The people believed that Baal granted increase to family, field, flocks and herds. This bride had forgotten that everything she had received had come from the hand of God, and so she began to focus on the provision itself, turning aside to worship Baal.

This is exactly what happens when the Church is long unopposed, as has largely been the case in America until recently. This has resulted in our making a tragic mistake: we have bowed our knee to the god of prosperity. Modern-day prophets of Baal have taught us that godliness is a means to financial gain—a false theology that has been an insidious snare to Christians throughout the generations. Sinners come in and are no longer challenged to forsake the pursuits of the natural life and heart, and therefore their affections remain firmly set on the things of this world. They continue to gravitate toward messages that focus on how they can be blessed, healthy, prosperous and socially relevant. Assured of the great destiny God has in store for them, they begin to embrace an offer of false hope and security.

What will happen to the prosperity crowd when the economy collapses? What will happen when those who were promised a promotion at work suddenly lose their job and can no longer pay the bills?

I believe we are going to see opposition clean up the house of God very quickly! A lot of the "big players" who have propagated these shallow messages are going to be cast to the wind, proven to be full of nothing but fluff. In the midst of it all, we will see that the Lord is determined to glorify His own name in this generation, just as He was in the days of Hosea:

> Therefore will I return, and take away my corn in the time thereof, and my wine. . . . I will also cause all her mirth to cease, her feast days, her new moons, and her sabbaths, and all her solemn feasts. And I will destroy her vines and her fig trees, whereof she hath said, These are my rewards that my lovers have given me. . . . I will

visit upon her the days of Baalim, wherein she burned incense to them, and she decked herself with her earrings and her jewels, and she went after her lovers, and forgat me, saith the LORD (Hos. 2:9,11-13).

The bottom line is that the Lord says, "I am going to take away all that has gripped her heart—everything that has not come from My hand and is not leading to Me. I will take it all away in a moment of time!"

How will this transpire in our day? The Lord has called for a famine! He is going to allow the tap of financial supply to run dry, calling for a financial downturn. In other words, we are about to have the carpet of false prosperity ripped out from under our feet as a church age. God is taking away everything that has brought us into a false confidence so that He might get the attention of His people as well as that of a lust-laden society.

Understand that there is no delight in the heart of God to do this. Nevertheless, He looks down and sees what was intended to be His heritage and says, "I cannot let this go on any longer. I cannot let these people continue to pursue a path that will lead them to destruction." That is why the Lord will shake it all until there is nothing left in this world to look to—nothing left in His Church but Him. I think the kindest thing the Lord can do for His Church is put us in a place where we *must* pray—a place where we need one another; where we finally realize that it doesn't matter what denomination the other person is from because we are all in the same boat together, fighting the same fight. That is the great kindness of the Lord.

Notice what the Lord says next: "Therefore, behold, I will allure her, and bring her into the wilderness, and speak comfortably unto her" (Hos. 2:14). Where? Into the wilderness! Why did He bring her there? To condemn her? No! To speak "comfortably" to her there. In the original Hebrew this word "comfortably" conveys the meaning of speaking tenderly, to the innermost parts of the heart. In other words, God will allure His Church into a barren place—away from the attractions and distractions of the age—so that He can finally speak straight to her heart.

"And I will give her her vineyards from thence, and the valley of Achor for a door of hope" (v. 15). The Valley of Achor is where an Israelite named Achan was judged by the camp of Joshua. The Israelites had just won a preliminary victory in the Promised Land. However, Achan was a covetous man who had gone into the battle with a heart gripped by the love of silver, gold, brass and clothing. He had taken some of these things and hidden them under his tent. Achan's sin ended up bringing a weakness upon the entire camp of Israel and ultimately meant defeat for the army of God.

It was in the Valley of Achor that Joshua fell on his face before God, only to have God tell him, "Get up. Why are you on your face? There is something forbidden in the camp, and it has taken away your strength" (see Josh. 7:10-12). It was in this Valley of Achor that the people rose up as one and declared, "No more! No more of this greed; no more of this covetousness." In the end, they stoned Achan and his family.

Do you think that was a bit severe? Have you ever wondered why the Holy Spirit killed Ananias and Sapphira at the very inception of the New Testament church (see Acts 5:1-11)? It was over the same issue that was being dealt with in the case of Achan. Ananias and Sapphira coveted money, and it was that same spirit that God knew would bring weakness into this early church.

I am not suggesting that poverty or want of resources should be the standard of God's people. God will bless His Church financially so that His work might be done on the earth. Money is not the problem; rather, it is the love of it and the shifting trust it brings. "For the love of money is the root of all evil: which while some coveted after, they have erred from the faith, and pierced themselves through with many sorrows" (1 Tim. 6:10).

God had to stop this spirit of covetousness in its tracks and cause it to lose its power—so Ananias and Sapphira dropped dead. If we will not deal with it, God will deal with it. If we will not put it in its rightful place, He will take it away. God will take His people to a place where these things are dealt with once and for all, even if that place is the wilderness.

God is doing this for the honor and glory of His Name. He is doing it to bring His Church back to strength again—to take away what has weakened her; to instill in her a right focus so that the power and virtue of Christ can begin to flow from her again. His bride will once again speak with authority in her mouth, direction in her eyes and gladness in her heart. It is the mercy of God that sends us into the wilderness. Yes, judgment is coming on the entire world, but mercy precedes and triumphs over judgment (see Jas. 2:13). God is willing to bring us to a place of realizing our true condition. How tragic it would be for us to live as if everything is fine only to discover that we missed the whole purpose, stopped short of the gateway to eternal life and lived a cultural Christianity with no reality in it. I have always thought it better to go to heaven hungry than to hell full.

If we choose not to humble ourselves and to allow the Lord to deal with these issues in our hearts now, one day we will have to face what will clearly stand as a just judgment. God has extended His hand of mercy not only over our society but over the entire world. That is why Paul plainly states in Romans that all men are without excuse. Once we know and understand this mercy of God yet still choose to reject it, judgment is just. That is why every tongue will be silenced except to say "Jesus Christ is Lord" when all humanity stands before the throne of God. God's mercy has been fully evident throughout scriptural history, extending right through to our day.

I am confident, however, that we can expect better things of God's people. The Lord goes on to describe His Bride in the wilderness:

> And she shall sing there, as in the days of her youth, and as in the day when she came up out of the land of Egypt. And it shall be at that day, saith the LORD, that thou shalt call me Ishi; and shalt call me no more Baali (Hos. 2:15-16).

In other words, the Lord is saying, "You will no longer call Me master. You will know Me in intimacy, and you will call Me husband. I will no longer merely be somebody who is calling you to do things just so you can be prospered by Me in the end. No! It will be an entirely different relationship—one that is much deeper. You will know My heart, and we will share an intimacy such as you never imagined to be possible. We will walk together as a bride and groom."

GOOD THINGS HAPPEN
IN BAD PLACES

Do you know why we do not have to be afraid of the coming days? Think of the time when Moses and Aaron stood before Pharaoh in order to deliver the Israelites from their bondage in Egypt. Moses boldly declared to Pharaoh, "We are all going—our children, our grandchildren, our young, our old and even our flocks and herds. All of us are going!" (see Exod. 10:9).

Where were they all going? They too were headed into the wilderness! It was a place where they would have to trust God for everything. Remember, it was in the wilderness that supernatural provision was discovered and manna first appeared to the children of Israel (see Deut. 8:2-3). It is in the place far away from where everyone is trusting in his own arm of strength and his own wisdom that suddenly supernatural provision becomes available. The Lord promises to provide, but we must first be taken to the place where God can make it appear.

Even when the prophet Elijah had the cry in his heart, "Oh, God, turn the heart of this nation back to You again!" God essentially replied to him, "Do you really want that to happen? Well, you are going to have to live beside a brook for a few years, because I am going to stop the rain. It is the only way I can get the attention of these people. I have to stop the rain, dry up the crops and cause a cry to be birthed in the nation" (see 1 Kings 17:2-4).

The rain did stop, and a severe famine came upon the land of Israel. Things soon became so unbearable that the people were forced to consider a contest of true and false spiritual power. All of Israel gathered at Mount Carmel, along with the prophets of Baal and the prophets of Asherah. Elijah stood before them and challenged the people, "How long halt ye between two opinions? if the LORD be God, follow him: but if Baal, then follow him" (1 Kings 18:21). So too will the people in our generation be faced with this decision.

If you have had the same cry in your heart as Elijah—you have been praying for deliverance for your family, your city, your nation—do not be surprised at how God answers that prayer. Elijah had to go through the famine with everybody else so that he could be there when the hearts of the people began to turn. In the same way, the Church of Jesus Christ will have to go through the same days of hardship that everyone else is going to face.

Natural men cannot comprehend these things. They are unable to see any value in going through a season of famine, for their eyes are fixed only on the hardship. They do not understand what God is doing behind the scenes, and they forget that His ways are higher than our ways. However, if we avoid the wilderness, we will never know the supernatural pathways of God. We will never fully understand that He can open up pathways of impossibility where natural people cannot walk—where those who feel they have to figure everything out cannot go.

So when you look around and see everything starting to fail, take heart! We are about to meet in the wilderness, and just as with the bride in the Song of Solomon, there is a bride in this generation who will come out of the wilderness, leaning upon her Beloved.

PART 2

DIVINE
DEPOSITS

3

MORE PRECIOUS
THAN GOLD

*In this you greatly rejoice, though now for a little while,
if need be, you have been grieved by various trials, that the
genuineness of your faith, being much more precious than gold
that perishes, though it is tested by fire, may be found to praise,
honor, and glory at the revelation of Jesus Christ.*

1 PETER 1:6-7, *NKJV*

UNSHAKABLE

The Scriptures speak of yet another occasion when the people of God had to endure a time of great famine: "Moreover he called for a famine upon the land: he brake the whole staff of bread" (Ps. 105:16). This famine that broke out over Egypt and Canaan in the days of Jacob was severe, yet before calling for the famine, the Lord "sent a man before them, even Joseph" (v. 17).

We all want to be the one whom the Lord sends ahead. How many of us are zealous to answer the Lord's call when He asks, "Whom shall I send?" Like Isaiah, we eagerly volunteer, "Here am I; send me!" (see Isa. 6:8). Yet we often do so with scant understanding of the ways of God. Suddenly we find ourselves in the fire, and we wonder why we are undergoing such intense suffering and constant trials.

Perhaps today you are experiencing betrayal, persecution, torment in your mind, trouble with your children, the loss of someone close to your heart, or some other experience that has left you with almost unspeakable pain. It has driven you to prayer where you ask, "Lord, is this really necessary? Can't You just take it away in a moment? Why the struggle? Why the fury?"

Notice how the passage continues: "Joseph, who was sold for a servant: whose feet they hurt with fetters: he was laid in iron: until the time that his word came: the word of the LORD tried him" (Ps. 105:17-19). The Hebrew word for "tried" is *seraph*, which means "to melt metal, to refine, to purge gold or silver by fire in order to separate it from the impurities in it." Here is what the Scripture was saying: God gave Joseph a promise, but until that promise became a reality, the Word of God led Joseph to a place where he was put through the fire and purged of everything within him that was unlike the heart of God.

God knew there would be a myriad of people who were going to need provision—not only Joseph's own family but also the nation where he lived. There would be people starving and without hope. The Lord wanted to put something in Joseph's hand that would bring deliverance to his generation, but He simply could not put this kind of treasure in the hands of an untested vessel.

I want to suggest to you that we are facing a similar situation in our time. As we head toward a season of hardship, have you ever considered that the Lord is sending you ahead as He did Joseph? Just as it is His mercy that is allowing all of us to go through a collective storm, so it is His mercy sending you ahead to prepare you so that He might put something in your hand for people who will be in need. However, that preparation process means that the Word of the Lord must try you as well.

The apostle Peter explained it this way:

> Wherein ye greatly rejoice, though now for a season, if need be, ye are in heaviness through manifold temptations: that the trial of your faith, being much more precious than of gold that perisheth, though it be tried with fire, might be found unto praise and honour and glory at the appearing of Jesus Christ (1 Pet. 1:6-7).

The trial of your faith! If you feel that you are going through the trial of your life, don't despair! God has seen fit to prepare you by taking you through the fire.

How appropriate it is that in an hour when many in the world are turning to gold investments, the Lord is preparing His people to emerge with something more precious than the gold of this earth that perishes. Interestingly, one of the most significant predictions that David Wilkerson made in *The Vision* is that "the price of gold is going to rise astronomically, but it will not be sustained over a long period of time. . . . Neither silver nor gold will offer real security. . . . Gold hoarders are going to get hurt—badly." In 1973, when *The Vision* was published, the price of gold was at $65 an ounce. At the publishing of this book, it is somewhere in the vicinity of at least twenty times that amount. All this really signifies is that people are making one last effort to hang onto whatever sustainability they think this world can offer. Although many consider gold to be a tangible asset, it will fail to offer any real or lasting security, and those who have made significant investments in gold will ultimately suffer great loss. Even the prophet Isaiah said that one day people would cast their gold and silver to the moles and bats, realizing that there is no stability or future in it (see Isa. 2:20).

While many in the world are scurrying to buy gold, those who are wise will consider the words of Jesus: "I counsel thee to buy of me gold tried in the fire" (Rev. 3:18).

What does this look like? To get a better idea, let's take a more detailed look at Joseph's journey.

A LONG JOURNEY TO THE PALACE

When Joseph was a young boy, he received a great promise from God. God revealed to Joseph through dreams that he would become a leader with great influence (see Gen. 37:5-9). Not only that, Joseph also was favored above all his brothers by his father, Jacob, who gave him a coat of many colors. And so Joseph embarked on his journey with a pretty coat and a promise.

A mark of immaturity still rested on Joseph at that point, however. He was rather boastful as he shared with his family the dreams he had of all of them bowing down to him. He still lacked understanding of the purpose of God's power and provision. In eager anticipation of seeing God's promise fulfilled, he neglected to realize that there would be unanticipated stops along the journey.

The first stop? A pit—a place of abandonment and betrayal. Out of jealousy, Joseph's brothers threw him into a pit and eventually sold him off to a band of Ishmaelite merchants for twenty pieces of silver. What greater betrayal could Joseph have faced? I don't think we can fully grasp his pain. How deeply it must have wounded his heart to know that this treachery had been done at the hand of his very own brothers.

Betrayal is perhaps one of the most difficult classrooms we have to go through in life. Yet we must remember it is also the road Christ traveled, so we cannot expect to escape it. I too have suffered some deep betrayals in my life. One case took me a full year to get through. I was betrayed in a manner that I never believed I would be. Not many were aware of the situation, but I wept a lot during that season. I understand that these things can hurt very deeply—the most severe wounds inflicted by people you have grown to love and trust over the years.

Perhaps, like Joseph, you started with a dream and vision to be used of God, only to discover that some people who were close to you did not believe in your dream. Or maybe they were envious that you were seemingly speaking about things of faith that they did not fully embrace or understand, and so they somehow sold you off.

The Bible tells us that Joseph was taken to Egypt and eventually sold to become a servant in Potiphar's house. At that point, it seems that Joseph decided to make the best of the situation—walking under authority, resisting temptation day after day and allowing God to flow through his life. God's favor upon him soon became so evident that Potiphar made Joseph his personal attendant, entrusting the charge of his entire household to him (see Gen. 39:3-4).

In return for acting righteously, however, Potiphar's wife falsely accused Joseph of wrongdoing, and he was thrown into prison. Despite the adverse circumstances he once again found himself in, Joseph continued to walk uprightly. The favor of the Lord was upon him, and the prison warden soon put Joseph in charge of all the prisoners. One day Joseph helped Pharaoh's chief cupbearer by interpreting a dream for him. Although Joseph urged the cupbearer to remember him, when the cupbearer ended up getting released from the prison and restored to his position before Pharaoh, he completely forgot about Joseph for two years! How often is that the case! The good we do for others goes unrequited, or we are left in a place where we are seemingly forgotten.

It is significant to note that throughout this time, Joseph was in a prison reserved for the king's prisoners (see Gen. 39:20). This reminds us that often there is no other way for us to be purged of our impurities except by being in the King's prison. In other words, God Himself is the One who brings us to difficult places in order to purify us of things that do not need to be in our lives. It is all part of the Lord's refining process. The word of the Lord is trying us, just as it tried Joseph.

GOD'S BOOT CAMP

Another meaning for the word "tried" used in Psalm 105:19 is "to be fitted for the battle." When we find ourselves on a long journey from the promise to the palace, it will be easy for us to lose heart along the way. That is why we must remember that the Lord is fitting us for the battle ahead.

Just as men and women are trained for battle once they join the military, there is a process that the Lord must take His people through in order to prepare them for the spiritual war that they either knowingly or unknowingly find themselves in. Let me give you an example that will help you gain a better perspective on the trials you may be going through now or will go through in days to come.

Shortly after my eldest son went off to boot camp to become a Marine, he began to send me letters—fairly desperate letters. He even reached out to the heavyweights, asking me to please get Pastor Dave and Elder So-and-So to pray for him! It was easy for me to empathize with his desperation once I went down to North Carolina and got a tour of what these young men and women had to go through.

Our country's military has procedures designed to make young men and women into soldiers. These tests and challenges are so severe that they are almost impossible to endure. These young people go in, believing they have the world by the tail, but not long into the process, they realize that their perspective is not true at all. Very soon they begin to send home letters of deep regret because they do not understand what is happening in their lives. They don't realize that all this hardship is necessary in order to prepare them to be soldiers. They are being trained to be obedient and to take orders; they are building stamina that will enable them to stand against insurmountable odds. They are being taught about unity and perseverance; fear is being driven out of their hearts. When they make it through to the end, our hearts are proud that such fine men and women have been raised up to represent our nation.

God desires the same end result for us as His Church. It requires us, however, to undergo intense training. We would all like to come into the kingdom of God, to hear from the Lord, to get filled with the Holy Spirit and then to move forward unhindered as we wield the sword of the Spirit. We would love to represent Christ and see a multitude of souls saved, walking unopposed as every power of darkness flees before us. In other words, like Joseph, we want to take the pretty coat and the promise and go straight to the palace full of God's provision.

However, we must understand that God often cannot fulfill the promise He has given us until His character and nature are formed in us. There can be great danger when any measure of truth and revelation about God that we have been given is not yet fully formed in us. For example, Moses asked to know God, and he was given an incredible revelation: "And the LORD passed by before him, and proclaimed, The LORD, The LORD God, merciful and gracious, longsuffering, and abundant in goodness and truth, keeping mercy for thousands, forgiving iniquity and transgression and sin. . ." (Exod. 34:6-7). But it was not long afterward that Moses, out of frustration, struck a rock and called the people he was leading a bunch of rebels. He misrepresented God, and because of it, he was not allowed to enter the Promised Land.

God knows that there is a deep work He must do in us in order that we might truly represent Him, so off to God's boot camp we go! My son's letters represent what many of our prayers are like when we find ourselves in these times of intense testing and trial. Could it be because we still have our own vision of how the kingdom of God should operate and so little awareness of God's procedure for leading the man or woman He is going to use?

Many people who rise to prominence in Christian circles have never been through God's training and testing. They stand before others, even with good intentions, but they misrepresent God because the human spirit is still very much in control in their lives. In reality they are still angry, fault-finding, intolerant and full of other things that originate from the human heart and have nothing at all to do with God. They are not complete in their understanding of Christ because they constantly did everything in their power to circumvent God's dealings with them.

That is what happens when you do not recognize that all along, your trials were part of God's boot camp. It was not man who opposed you; the mercy of God allowed you to be opposed. The mercy of God brought you to the place where you are right now. It was God who allowed the voices to be raised against you. He easily could have slapped His hand over their mouths and stopped them from speaking, but He chose not to. He is in the process of doing a deep work within you, refining your faith. In the end, you will be glad He did.

So what happened to Joseph after the Word of the Lord tried him? "The king sent and loosed him; even the ruler of the people, and let him go free. He made him lord of his house, and ruler of all his substance" (Ps. 105:20-21). God does not forget His promises or His purpose for our lives. There is a moment coming when you will finally understand why difficult things have happened. That is the "loosing." You will understand that you and I simply do not have the strength of character to represent Christ until the Lord forms Himself in us—until He becomes our source of supply and strength, until we have been broken and remade into the image of the One who came to this world and went to a cross for your sake and for mine.

Once you begin to see how necessary this trial of your faith is, your heart will be inclined to believe God through it all, no matter how long the journey to the fulfillment of His promises. If you are willing to allow God to take you through the fire now, even though the economy may fail in the near future, you will surely emerge with something more precious than gold.

4

SOME THINGS CANNOT BE LEARNED FROM A BOOK

*I have learned in any and all circumstances
the secret of facing every situation.*

PHILIPPIANS 4:12, *AMP*

UNSHAKABLE

I n 1989 I traveled to eastern Canada, conducting evangelistic meetings and testifying of the goodness of God in various churches that were in need of encouragement. Now when you return home from any season of traveling, you usually expect to find some personal rest and comfort. The last thing you expect to find is your house burned to the ground.

The fire department said it was one of the most incredible fires they had ever seen. Other than the chimney, there was absolutely nothing left. Everything had collapsed into the foundation, and not a single wall was left standing. It was a complete and total destruction of my home.

Standing there in my yard, memory after memory began to flash through my mind. Oh, the joy of the Lord that used to fill that home! What laughter and praise would resound throughout the house as we all gathered around the old piano. I could picture the steps that led up to the living room—the place where I sat one day with my guitar. Newly saved, filled with the Holy Spirit and absolutely in love with God, I struck the chord of E and wrote a song called "I Love You, Jesus."

I glanced over to where the kitchen used to be—the place where my wife and I were called into the ministry. It was also in that kitchen that the Holy Spirit met me in such a sovereign way one day. It was an encounter with God that brought a deeper reverential fear into my heart, beyond anything I had ever known in my lifetime.

God's provision there over the years was clearly evident; the blessing of God touched our home on every side. It was a place where many people were taken into shelter. One winter we had seventeen people in our home—a single mother and her two children, a pastor who needed shelter in order to continue the work of God, and several others who found themselves in difficult situations. It was in this house that we learned to have faith to trust God for the impossible. We not only fed people beyond our natural means, but we were fed supernaturally as well.

And now suddenly everything was gone. All the comforts, all the pictures of our children, all the work I had done to renovate the old log farmhouse, everything that we had accumulated up until that point—all gone.

At that moment, it would have been easy for me to stand in my yard and cry out, "God, is *this* how You reward me for taking in the homeless? Is this what I get for praising You, for living for You, for traveling to testify about You? You decide to take away everything that we have?" The enemy's prime time for planting doubts in our mind regarding God's goodness is right in the midst of our most intense trials. That is when we must make a choice.

As I stood before the embers of my house, I chose to trust God. I chose to believe that everything He allows is for a reason. In hindsight, I now realize that God knew I would be moving to New York. He also knew that certain things had to happen; certain things needed to be taken away from me. A deep trust had to be birthed within my heart, a personal revelation of God's keeping power—and there was no other way to develop that kind of trust except through the fire. God knew that I would later be called to stand in far more difficult circumstances, so now was the time for faith to be worked in my heart.

GOD'S INDUSTRY STANDARD

As we saw in the previous chapter, there is no escaping the fire if we expect to be used of God. Of course, not all of us will have our faith tested in the fire quite as literally as I did. That day only one thing of my house was left standing—the fireplace with its chimney. It seemed to stand as a grave reminder that one day everything that can be shaken will be shaken.

The only reason that this part of the structure withstood the fire was because it had been specifically designed to do so. It was not made of ordinary material but was built with previously tested and proven substances that met required industry standards. While ordinary mortar will begin to crumble, crack and dry out, fireplace mortar gets stronger the more it is touched by heat.

The brick that was there had been laboratory tested, and it was proven to be able to endure a thousand fires. Suppose a contractor, after he finished building a fireplace in your home, said to you, "We got this brick cheap, but it looks great. It comes with a pamphlet full of lots of promises. And by the way, it has never been tested in the fire." Can you imagine? You'd better be prepared to run!

Yet think about the number of people today who are building a Christian life on fancy, cheap bricks and pamphlets of empty promises. They have spent their lives seeking ease and comfort, avoiding every difficulty, and therefore their faith has never been tested in the fire. But very shortly it will be. As the Scripture says, "Every man's work shall be made manifest: for the day shall declare it, because it shall be revealed by fire; and the fire shall try every man's work of what sort it is" (1 Cor. 3:13). In other words, God says, "I will know every man's work, of what it is truly made. The ingredients of the inner core shall be revealed, and we will see, when difficulty comes, what is left standing in My house that has claimed to be part of My kingdom."

The Lord has His own industry standards, for He is concerned about the Christian having more than exterior beauty. In God's people there must be an interior structure that allows us to go through difficulties and buffetings. Some of the prettiest, most well-polished Christians are going to head for the hills in the coming days because of what we will face. It will be the ones who may not be eloquent, who are not well-known personalities, who do not look like much to the natural eye who will be left standing. They will emerge with a word from God and a confidence in Him because they have been tested.

This held true in the life of Joseph. Let's look now at another example of someone who certainly went through one fiery trial after another and yet was able to "withstand in the evil day, and having done all, to stand" (Eph. 6:13).

STRENGTHENED IN THE FIRE

It was the apostle Paul who penned those words to exhort the believers in Ephesus. Another translation says it this way: "Then after the battle you will still be standing firm" (Eph. 6:13, *NLT*). Of course, there would not be much weight to Paul's words had he himself not gone through the fire and ultimately been able to stand.

From the very onset of his ministry, the apostle Paul was entrusted with great suffering and trials. Shortly after the Lord stopped Paul on the road to Damascus, He appeared in a vision to a man named Ananias and told him to pray for Paul: "For he is a chosen vessel unto me, to bear my name before the Gentiles, and kings, and the children of Israel: for I will shew him how great things he must suffer for my name's sake" (Acts 9:15-16). Paul clearly understood that he was appointed by God to be His witness, thus he embraced the suffering that accompanied this call. In fact, he even went so far as to regard suffering as "fellowship." Notice what he said to the Philippian church: "That I may know him, and the power of his resurrection, and the fellowship of his sufferings, being made conformable unto his death" (Phil. 3:10).

It is tragic that the truth about suffering in the Christian life is largely neglected in much of today's theology. I find it appalling that there are even places where people completely discount Paul's life and the things he had to go through. Instead, they use the words of Paul to somehow convince people that suffering and trials should not be part of the Christian experience. It is almost inconceivable that the church could be inundated with such an errant gospel, especially as we see in the Scriptures that Paul certainly did not try to hide his trials from the early church:

> For we would not, brethren, have you ignorant of our trouble which came to us in Asia, that we were pressed out of measure, above strength, insomuch that we despaired even of life: but we had the sentence of death in ourselves, that we should not trust in ourselves, but in God which raiseth the dead (2 Cor. 1:8-9).

Paul was constantly delivered into places in which he could not have survived in his own strength. He experienced suffering and trials to such a degree that without the infusion of Christ's life within, he could not have endured in his own human ability. However, Paul possessed an inner core that proves to us today that, by the life of Christ within them, ordinary people are able to withstand all the adversity and opposition they encounter. And just as fireplace mortar is strengthened through increased exposure to heat, so the true Christian—no matter what God allows to be brought against us or allows the enemy to throw our way—will be strengthened by the fire. Our faith becomes deeper each time we are tested.

This means that you should not expect the trials to stop simply because you think your character has been adequately refined and you are ready to rightly represent Christ! Paul ended up writing from jail and was ultimately beheaded, which tells us that his suffering did not cease until the end of his days.

I HAVE LEARNED

What were these trials that Paul endured over the course of his life? He lists some of them for us:

Of the Jews five times received I forty stripes save one. Thrice was I beaten with rods, once was I stoned, thrice I suffered shipwreck, a night and a day I have been in the deep; in journeyings often, in perils of waters, in perils of robbers, in perils by mine own countrymen, in perils by the heathen, in perils in the city, in perils in the wilderness, in perils in the sea, in perils among false brethren; in weariness and painfulness, in watchings often, in hunger and thirst, in fastings often, in cold and nakedness (2 Cor. 11:24-27).

How many of us would want the testimony of this man? Yet how many of us desire the revelation that he was given!

Through his continued trials, Paul received not only strength but an ever-increasing personal revelation of Christ. Now keep in mind that suffering does not make one man holier than another, nor does it mean that if you do not suffer, you do not know anything about God. Nevertheless, those who have suffered tend to possess an intimate knowledge—a revelation of the keeping and sustaining power of God that is often hardly understood by the casual observer.

How else was Paul able to see this magnificence of God that he wrote about to the church in Ephesus? "Oh, if you could see what I see! That you could see Him sitting at the right hand of the Father, far above every principality and power and name that can be named; that you could see God who has put all things under His feet; that you could see that He is the head and we are the body, that He is the fullness, that He fills all in all" (see Eph. 1:18-23).

How could Paul say, "I have learned, in whatsoever state I am, therewith to be content. I know both how to be abased, and I know how to abound: every where and in all things I am instructed both to be full and to be hungry, both to abound and to suffer need. I can do all things through Christ which strengtheneth me" (Phil. 4:11-13)? In other words, "In all my circumstances, I will not be overwhelmed, for I have learned that Christ in me is a victorious strength over everything that I have faced and will have to face in this life!"

Paul did not come to know these things by study nor merely by divine revelation. Yes, he was a man who had studied and knew the Scriptures, who was a calculated debater of truth everywhere he went. He even said that he was lifted up into the presence of God, caught up to the third heaven and given such incredible revelation that it required a thorn in his flesh to keep him from becoming proud (see 2 Cor. 12:2-7). However, all his study and all this revelation did not produce this knowledge in him. It is the suffering man who comes to the depth of understanding that Paul had gained.

Paul was a man who desperately needed God every day, every step of the journey. He was able to make these phenomenal statements in sincerity because he had gone through the fire and personally experienced the keeping power of God. The words he spoke and wrote became words of God in him that had been proven. Who could argue against them after all that he had been through?

His life clearly illustrated the fact that people with experience have much more weight in their speech than people who just have knowledge. We can study the Word of God, we can memorize it, and we can quote it everywhere we go. But study only exposes us to truth. It is experience, particularly through times of suffering, that brings us to the place where the real power of that truth becomes known. And so we see a great difference between the person who says, "I know the Scripture," versus the person who, like Paul, says, "I have *learned*."

It is one thing to have a 19-year-old Bible school student get up and testify, "I am telling you that no matter what trial you are going to experience, God is going to bring you through!" It may be nice, and it certainly is true, but there will not be much weight to his words. On the other hand, when someone like Pastor Ben Crandall assures us that we are going to make it, it carries much weight. Ben Crandall, who is in his late eighties, is our most senior pastor—a man who has lived through many tests and trials over the years. He even had the police come to his door at two o'clock one morning bearing the news that his daughter had just been killed in a car accident. Yet now when he gets up and says, "I am here to tell you that God is able to bring you through your trial," a whole force of heaven comes behind those words because this man has walked through the fire, and he has not given up on God.

It is important to realize that God is sending you through the fire, preparing to put something in your hand as He did Joseph—not as somebody who just knows but as somebody who has *learned*. If you take the easy way out, you will never know this. You will know *about* it, but you will not know it. That is why you must go through the trials—that you may know Christ.

ACCESS GRANTED

After Paul had endured many trials, it was as if God said, "Now I can put a quill in that hand. Now that hand can be moved by the Holy Spirit so that the words in My heart can be put on paper for future generations." The incredible encouragement found within Paul's inspired letters still speaks to us today:

> He comforts us in all our troubles so that we can comfort others. When they are troubled, we will be able to give them the same comfort God has given us. For the more we suffer for Christ, the more God will shower us with his comfort through Christ. Even when we are weighed down

with troubles, it is for your comfort and salvation! For when we ourselves are comforted, we will certainly comfort you. Then you can patiently endure the same things we suffer. We are confident that as you share in our sufferings, you will also share in the comfort God gives us (2 Cor. 1:4-7, *NLT*).

These words of Paul reveal another truth about suffering: it fills individuals with something of Christ that enables them to reach people who might otherwise never understand the grace of the gospel. It grants them access into the deepest inner prisons of their generation—places no one else can go except those who have personally experienced God's comfort in the midst of their own trials. That means that if you are going to be able to comfort the sorrowing in the coming days, you yourself must first receive comfort from God.

Years ago when I was pastoring in a small town in Canada, we met a young Christian woman who lived this truth. She was one of those people who seemed to experience heartache after heartache. Some time after her husband left her and their four children, her beautiful four-year-old daughter began to appear ill. It turned out that the child had leukemia, and the disease took her life. I cannot begin to describe the incredible anguish—

the wailing and the depth of sorrow—that came into that mother's heart.

A few months later, a lady in our community was told that she had only a short while to live. She was not a Christian, and she shut everyone out, choosing to live in total darkness and despair. Many of us attempted to visit and encourage her, but she refused to open her door to anyone. Until one day. This young mother went over to the woman's house and said, "Wait! Before you shut the door, I want to tell you that I recently lost my daughter to leukemia. I understand what you're going through." The door opened, and the young mother ended up not only leading this woman to Christ but also walking with her through her difficult days until she went home to be with the Lord.

There are times when we have to ask: What is the value of a soul? Is it worth it? What price did God pay for a soul?

I hope you are beginning to see how unwise we are if we live only to escape every difficulty—if the gospel we pursue is somehow only for the sake of making us comfortable! It will never touch our generation, because people do not live there.

It is just as Paul wrote to Timothy: "The husbandman that laboureth must be first partaker of the fruits.

Consider what I say; and the Lord give thee understanding in all things" (2 Tim. 2:6-7). When he was approaching the end of his life, Paul spoke to Timothy in
the context of suffering. He was saying, "God has brought
me through many trials, and He has kept me. Timothy,
you must go through it first. If you want to preach to
the people that they can get to the other side of the
storm, you have to go through the storm first. You have
to be the first partaker of faith, reaching a point when all
you have left is faith." So rather than constantly looking for a way out of our trials, we must learn to walk
through them in the strength of God. It is often in these
places of great darkness that we come to know Him the
most intimately. Soon we will emerge with words that
have weight, and we will be granted access to those who
are hurting in this generation.

I remember going for a long jog one morning shortly
after our house burned down. At that time we didn't
even have sufficient clothing for our children. I had previously given away the little savings I had, so I had no financial fallback and no real plan for the future. Yet the
words of Jesus in the Gospel of Matthew suddenly came
to my mind: "But seek ye first the kingdom of God, and
his righteousness; and all these things shall be added
unto you" (Matt. 6:33). I said to God, "Lord, according

to Your Word I have sought You, I have sought Your kingdom, and I have sought Your righteousness. You promised that all I need will be added to me, so I am simply going to take You at Your Word." At that point, I made the choice to put away the fear of tomorrow. Suddenly peace flooded my heart.

God did exactly as He had promised. He added all things unto me, and He did it sovereignly. I did not say a word to anyone, but the story of our loss somehow spread everywhere—throughout our community and even to communities beyond. Suddenly people began responding, and churches that I had never even been to ended up taking offerings for us. God gave back to us everything that had been lost. And after the trial was all over, the Lord told me, "I needed to show you that I can take it all away, and I can give it all back. It is all in My hands." I too have *learned* that God is my keeper, and I am confident that He will keep you as well.

5

A RIGHT RESPONSE

*Now My soul is troubled and distressed, and what
shall I say? Father, save Me from this hour
[of trial and agony]? But it was for this very purpose
that I have come to this hour [that I might
undergo it]. [Rather, I will say,] Father, glorify
(honor and extol) Your [own] name!*

JOHN 12:27-28, *AMP*

UNSHAKABLE

At a pastors' conference in one of the former Eastern Bloc countries, God had put it on my heart to speak on the purpose of suffering in the Christian life. Approximately 1,000 pastors were in attendance, and the message I was about to share was one that I had battled with beforehand. "Lord, these men and women suffer already. Why can't I bring a word of encouragement or talk about some kind of blessing instead? Why have You put this message on my heart?"

Nevertheless, on the first day of the conference, I went ahead and preached what I knew the Lord had given me—only to be met with a silence that was almost eerie. When I was finished, the pastors in that room simultaneously fell on their knees and began to weep. Initially I thought, *Oh, God, I've brought more despair to their hearts when I should have encouraged them!*

After the meeting, one of their leaders approached me and essentially said, "Pastor, you don't know what has happened today. All this time we thought that God was angry with us. We have been put out of our jobs because we are Christians. It is hard for us to pay our bills. Some of us could barely even afford gas to come to this conference. Yet we watch television programs from your country and get the impression that if we are children of God, we should be wealthy and abounding. So when we suffer, we assume God must be angry with us."

At that point I realized that they had actually fallen on their knees, weeping for joy! They finally understood that what was happening in their lives was not God's punishment. On the contrary, He was preparing them to be able to stand in the days ahead.

A ROOT OF BITTERNESS

Sadly, many people fail to understand the purpose of suffering and trials in the Christian life. As a result, they often end up under condemnation, thinking that God is punishing them, or sinking in despair during their trials. That is why it is imperative for us to remember that God has a divine purpose behind all our hardships. This is particularly important for those who were once given a promise or vision from God and have since yielded themselves to be used for His purposes. How distant and impossible the promise might appear once they begin to be put through the fire!

Think about it. Had Joseph not at least marginally understood that the trials he faced were all a necessary part of the journey, he easily could have slipped into despondency during his thirteen years of opposition. Or think of Paul having to endure violent responses from crowds, betrayals, shipwrecks, isolation . . . things that must have caused an overwhelming sense of despair to begin pushing at the door of his heart.

Beware if you ever find despair beginning to overwhelm you, for on the coattails of despair is an enemy far more dangerous: bitterness. It is the feeling of being wronged, betrayed and abandoned—especially by God. Many people reach this point in their trials and begin to question God's commitment to them. "God, I once had such great hope, such faith in Your promises. You said that Your power was going to emanate from my life. But now I have no strength or courage left. I feel betrayed and abandoned. Why have You forsaken me?" This cry has entered into the heart of many Christians today, whether or not they have the courage to articulate it. Their heart is failing in the time of testing, and they cannot see the hand of God anymore.

This is exactly what the enemy wants—to draw you into such deep despair that he can easily sow bitterness into your life. The writer of Hebrews warns of this very thing: "Lest any root of bitterness springing up trouble you, and thereby many be defiled" (Heb. 12:15). Notice that it will be many, not only a few, who will be defiled by bitterness.

"God, I trusted you!" these disillusioned Christians will cry. No! They didn't trust God; they trusted their own view of what their life was going to look like when they came into ministry. Somehow the place where they find themselves does not line up with their original impression of what walking with Christ would be like. Soon, when things seem to be unbearable, they become offended with God. They ultimately open their hearts to the whisperings of the evil one as he accuses the faithfulness of God.

"God, you have failed me!" No! God has not failed them. They failed to go beyond the surface of Scripture to learn what it really means to walk with Christ. They failed to embrace the truths that promise to sustain those who are determined to walk in the footsteps of their Master.

FAITHFUL AFFLICTIONS

What incredible truth we find in the riddle that Samson once posed to the Philistines after he had killed a young lion that roared against him: "Out of the eater came forth meat, and out of the strong came forth sweetness" (Judg. 14:14). In other words, out of what should have destroyed me came honey that I took home to my family, and it became strength for those who needed it. That is how it works in God's kingdom—things will rise against you that would seemingly destroy you, yet out of them God will bring a sweetness and nourishment not only for your life but for the lives of others. So do not let your own heart or any power of evil suggest to you that you are going to be triumphed over. Declare God to be faithful in your trial, and realize deep down that He will never fail nor forsake you. The Lord God has tied the honor of His own name to His commitment to keep you.

In light of these truths, have you ever come to the place of just thanking God, even in the midst of your trial? Many people are fixed on praying, "Oh, Lord, deliver me from my enemies! Take me out of this hardship!" Yet have you ever thought of thanking the Lord for where He has you, for the strength He is planting within you, for the deposit of His life in you for the future? Have you ever considered thanking God for entrusting you with some suffering, that you might walk as Christ did?

As Paul said, "For unto you it is given in the behalf of Christ, not only to believe on him, but also to suffer for his sake" (Phil. 1:29). No matter what adverse circumstances you find yourself in today, be thankful that the Lord is bringing you into places of fire where everything unlike Christ is being purged. He is working out His purposes in your life and fitting you to represent Him in this generation.

Over the years, I have learned this lesson of thanking God for the hard times, not just the good times. I have come to realize that the trials produce something in me that the good times don't. The trials mold something within me that the good times could never form in my heart. The trials show me my need of God, revealing to me that my own inability can be overcome by the grace, goodness and power of my Savior. The trials purify my faith. I thank God for the mountaintops, for I have had some wonderful experiences there. However, the growth of my character as a Christian has predominantly come in the valley. I would rather not go there, but it is in the valley that I have found strength that only God can give. It is in the valley that I have walked into something of Christ's life that now overflows from within me for others.

Years ago, when my family and I first came to New York City, I began to grow very sick and developed asthma. In fact, I could hardly breathe sometimes, having headaches so fierce that I eventually had to get an oxygen tank. We later found out that the home we had moved into was laced with toxic mold. By the time it was discovered, the attic of this only twelve-year-old home was so black that we could not even see the wood siding.

I remember having to use the oxygen tank just to be able to do my devotions in the morning. "The devil is after you," was the general conclusion of those around me. Yet in my heart I began to hear something from the Lord: *I have allowed this.* The Lord led me to Psalm 119, where He speaks of afflictions:

Before I was afflicted I went astray: but now have I kept thy word (v. 67).

It is good for me that I have been afflicted; that I might learn thy statutes (v. 71).

I know, O LORD, that thy judgments are right, and that thou in faithfulness hast afflicted me (v. 75).

You may be struggling today, perhaps in the biggest battle of your life. But when you begin to grasp this truth—that afflictions help us to learn God's ways and walk in them—you will begin to thank Him for the trial He has allowed in your life. It is evidence of His faithfulness. Without it you would never reach the depth of understanding that He wants to release into your life.

I recall walking down the street one day, so short of breath that I began to stagger. Suddenly the Lord spoke to my heart, "Resident within you is the capability of doing great harm to the church in New York City; therefore I am going to deal with you so that you will never do that. I am going to cause you to become dependent upon Me. Your feet will be nailed to the floor so that you will not have the liberty to travel around the world and simply do whatever you please. You will be aware that your strength is limited. If the Holy Spirit is not carrying you, you will not have enough gas in your physical tank to go more than ten miles, and you will know it." To this day, I know that I cannot accept every invitation I receive. If the Holy Spirit is not leading me to do it—if He is not sustaining me—it can take me up to three weeks to recover from a trip.

God is faithful, and He knows what we need. He knows what must happen in our lives, which valleys you and I have to walk through. He knows what opposition has to come against us in order to make us a people who can stand in this generation and truly represent Jesus Christ in these last days of time.

A SONG IS BIRTHED

Learning to thank God for the trials is critical not only for our sake but for those around us. This was another truth that Paul understood about suffering: people are watching. Every trial we go through is an opportunity for the testimony of Christ to be made manifest in our lives.

Do you remember what happened to Paul and Silas when they were in Philippi? Although they were innocent of wrongdoing, they were rejected, severely beaten and then thrust into the inner prison where their feet were clamped in the stocks (see Acts 16:22-24). In other words, through no fault of their own, Paul and Silas were brought into a dark, uncomfortable place to dwell among those who were full of despair.

It was a place that reflects the situation that many people in society now find themselves—a place of extreme oppression and hopelessness. Don't be surprised in the coming days if you find yourself in a similar place. The Lord knows that sometimes the only way the individuals around us can be reached is if He entrusts a similar suffering to some of His own. That way our hearts are softened, and we can begin to understand where they live, identify with the pain they are going through and ultimately walk alongside them.

What did Paul and Silas do when they found themselves in that inner prison? Did they complain about the injustice done to them? Were they overcome with bitterness, questioning God? No! Suddenly, cutting straight through the darkness and despair of that midnight hour came their songs of praise to God! As a result, the whole foundation of the devil's plan to swallow this society of prisoners in their own pain was broken. "Suddenly there was a great earthquake, so that the foundations of the prison were shaken: and immediately all the doors were opened, and every one's bands were loosed" (Acts 16:26). Paul and Silas's choice to praise God in the midst of suffering resulted in liberty not only for themselves but for others as well.

Like Paul and Silas, many of God's saints have gone through incredible adversity over the course of their lives, yet out of that adversity a song was born—a song that had the power to touch their generation and, in many cases, generations to come as well. In his book entitled *Then Sings My Soul,* Robert J. Morgan gives us the classic example of Horatio G. Spafford:

> When the great Chicago fire consumed the Windy City in 1871, Horatio G. Spafford, an attorney heavily invested in real estate, lost a for-

tune. About that time, his only son, age 4, succumbed to scarlet fever. Horatio drowned his grief in work, pouring himself into rebuilding the city and assisting the 100,000 who had been left homeless.

In November of 1873, he decided to take his wife and daughters to Europe. Horatio was close to D. L. Moody and Ira Sankey, and he wanted to visit evangelistic meetings in England, then enjoy a vacation.

When an urgent matter detained Horatio in New York, he decided to send his wife, Anna, and their four daughters, Maggie, Tanetta, Annie, and Bessie, on ahead. As he saw them settled into a cabin aboard the luxurious French liner *Ville du Havre*, an unease filled his mind, and he moved them to a room closer to the bow of the ship. Then he said good-bye, promising to join them soon.

During the small hours of November 22, 1873, as the *Ville du Havre* glided over smooth seas, the passengers were jolted from their bunks. The ship had collided with an iron sailing vessel, and water poured in like Niagara . . . Within two hours, the mighty ship vanished beneath the waters. The 226 fatalities included Maggie, Tanetta, Annie, and Bessie. Mrs. Spafford was found nearly unconscious, clinging to a piece of the wreckage. When the 47 survivors landed in Cardiff, she cabled her husband: "Saved Alone."

Horatio immediately booked passage to join his wife. En route, on a cold December night, the captain called him aside and said, "I believe we are now passing over the place where the *Ville du Havre* went down." Spafford went to his cabin but found it hard to sleep. He said to himself, "It is well: the will of God be done."

He later wrote his famous hymn based on those words.[1]

God often allows suffering in your life to draw you to a place of knowing Him intimately—so intimately that even in your darkest hour, you will raise your hands and praise Him. After all, have you ever considered that battles may arise in your life because it is the only way God can speak to somebody around you? Your co-worker or neighbor may never open a Bible, but they will certainly watch your response in the midst of difficult times. Sooner or later they will have to consider, *This person is going through the same trials and difficulties that I'm go-*

ing through now, but they are praising God! How can that be possible? That is when people will start to be released from the captivity of darkness. It is just as the psalmist David wrote:

> I waited patiently for the LORD; and he inclined unto me, and heard my cry. He brought me up also out of an horrible pit, out of the miry clay, and set my feet upon a rock, and established my goings. And he hath put a new song in my mouth, even praise unto our God: many shall see it, and fear, and shall trust in the LORD (Ps. 40:1-3).

He has put a song in my mouth, and many shall see it. The verse does not say many shall *hear* it—it says that they shall *see* it. They will see you walking into your office or in your community, well aware that you are going through adversity, and recognize that for some reason you have not lost your confidence in God. You will be walking with strength and peace that is supernatural. Those going through similar struggles will have an inner witness that the Lord is with you—that only the hand of God Almighty could sustain you through such trials.

As difficult as this may be, I encourage you today to ask the Lord for great grace to respond with a thankful heart during times of trial. Learn now to thank Him for the hard times. Count Him worthy of praise even in the midst of your pain; declare His goodness even when you find yourself in situations that you don't understand. Thank God that He has counted you faithful to be brought into the place of trial where ordinary people without the Spirit of God would not survive. After all, how can you show that the gospel is extraordinary if an ordinary man can live it? For this reason, all through the Scriptures we see that God has led His choicest servants into seasons of impossibility where only divine strength would be sufficient.

Yes, walking through such seasons will be difficult. But remember, you will never know victory if there is no battle. You cannot obtain faith until you start winning victories. Faith does not come simply by memorizing Scripture, as good as that is. Rather, the classrooms you must be trained in are living and real. I have personally lived this, yet God has never failed me—not once. I cannot lay a single accusation at His throne. There were times when I thought I could not go on another day, but the Lord took my hand and gave me the strength to continue, all the while building a bank of faith in my heart.

In the same way, He will be faithful to you through every trial. The way to build your faith is by allowing

God to walk you through the flood and through the fire—all the while being careful not to lose your song. With every victory you will find a new measure of faith. Another deposit of trust in the Lord will be put into your heart. It will be a testimony; something of worth that you will now be able to impart to others. In the next chapter, we will see what kind of investments God intends for us to make with those deposits.

Note

1. Robert J. Morgan, *Then Sings My Soul*, vol. 1 (Nashville, TN: Thomas Nelson, 2003), p. 185.

PART 3

UNLOCKING AN ENDLESS SUPPLY

6

WHERE SHALL I INVEST?

Is not this the fast that I have chosen?
to loose the bands of wickedness, to undo the heavy burdens,
and to let the oppressed go free, and that ye break every yoke?
Is it not to deal thy bread to the hungry,
and that thou bring the poor that are cast out to thy house?
when thou seest the naked, that thou cover him;
and that thou hide not thyself from thine own flesh?

ISAIAH 58:6-7

UNSHAKABLE

The instability of today's global market has left people hard-pressed to find the wisest places to invest. After all, there are no investment strategies that can guarantee dividends in the midst of an uncertain future . . . except one. The Lord offers a divine principle that, if heeded, will sustain His people in the coming days. It is simply this: learn to invest in people.

We must never forget that people are the focus of God. He came into the world to redeem fallen humanity—to save you and to save me. He came for no other reason. He did not come to make us feel better about ourselves or to give us a bigger slice of the socioeconomic pie. As the well-known verse tells us, "For God so loved the world, that he gave his only begotten Son" (John 3:16). He found the redemption of our souls worth the price of His own blood and the keeping and consecrating of our lives worth the deposit of His very own Spirit. What an incredible investment He has made in humanity! If we truly share His heart, other people ought to be our focus also.

This concept is contrary to our natural instincts, particularly in a time of calamity. Our entire focus turns inward and our tendency is to withdraw our hand from doing good and instead begin to cry out about ourselves. When the disciples found themselves in the midst of a storm and saw that Jesus was asleep at the back of the boat, they began to cry out, "Master, do You not care if we perish?" (see Mark 4:35-39).

They completely neglected the fact that other little ships were traveling in the same storm with them, also attempting to get to the other side of the sea. The disciples were the only ones in the storm who visibly saw God and knew that He was with them. You would think that their cry would be, "Master, wake up. There are people out there in little boats who are perishing. We have You here with us; You have told us that we are going to the other side, and that is sufficient. But others don't have You with them. You must do something!" Of course, other people were not their chief concern at the moment. Usually the last thing on our minds during a calamity is investing in other people. However, this is what will actually sustain us—giving to others, particularly in our own time of need.

INSTRUCTIONS FOR THE FAMINE

Let's return to the story of Elijah for a moment. Before the confrontation between Elijah and the false prophets took place on the top of Mount Carmel, the Lord gave Elijah specific instructions, since he would have to go through the same famine as everyone else. Here is what the Lord said to him:

> Get thee hence, and turn thee eastward, and hide thyself by the brook Cherith, that is before Jordan. And it shall be, that thou shalt drink of the brook; and I have commanded the ravens to feed thee there (1 Kings 17:3-4).

Imagine being in Elijah's position. He had just declared that there would be no rain for the next few years, and now he heard God telling him, "Go to this brook and camp out there. Birds are going to come and feed you." How many of us would rather come up with a plan that sounds a bit more logical? Yet at these very moments we must remember that God's ways are not our ways; His thoughts are higher than our thoughts.

After a while, Elijah probably got rather comfortable living by the brook. In his heart he may have thought, *This is wonderful! The rain has stopped, and God is preparing the nation to turn back to Him. But as for me, I have this refreshing water here every day. Not to mention that I don't even have to cook! Ravens just appear and suddenly I have roast rabbit! God left me here in a safe place. I am going from here straight to Mount Carmel.*

Elijah represents a type of person today who lies by a spiritual brook—opening the Bible every day, enjoying the cool water and supernatural provision of God anytime he wants. Meanwhile, despair is all around him—people are confused; others are losing their jobs. Yet all the while he simply concludes, *I'm just going to ride out the storm here.*

If that was Elijah's plan, it certainly backfired. "And it came to pass after a while, that the brook dried up, because there had been no rain in the land" (1 Kings 17:7). Right before Elijah's eyes, the brook started to narrow, and a troubling began. *God, what are You doing? I thought You were going to feed and comfort me! What's going on here?*

We may camp around the promises of God for a season, but there always comes a point when God must provoke us to move on and respond to the cry of those around us. Now that even his water supply was shut off, Elijah received further instructions from the Lord:

And the word of the LORD came unto him, saying, Arise, get thee to Zarephath, which belongeth to Zidon, and dwell there: behold, I have commanded a widow woman there to sustain thee. So he arose and went to Zarephath. And when he came to the gate of the city, behold, the widow woman was there gathering of sticks: and he called to her, and said, Fetch me, I pray thee, a little water in a vessel, that I may drink. And as she was going to fetch it, he called to her, and said, Bring me, I pray thee, a morsel of bread in thine hand. And she said, As the LORD thy God liveth, I have not a cake, but an handful of meal in a barrel, and a little oil in a cruse: and, behold, I am gathering two sticks, that I may go in and dress it for me and my son, that we may eat it, and die (1 Kings 17:8-12).

At that point, Elijah may have been wondering, *How in the world is this woman going to provide for me? She does not even have enough for herself. In her own mind, she and her son only have a day left to live. Lord, are You sure? Aren't there any people in Israel who have something left in their cupboards? Is this really part of Your divine plan?* Notice that the Lord had told him, "I have commanded her to sustain you." Yet when Elijah got there, it was as if the widow was not even aware of this. So how exactly was this command given to her?

I believe it was simply this: the Lord was saying, "I have put it in her heart to listen to you."

The widow *was* ready to listen. By the time Elijah reached her, she did not have enough provision for even one more day. Her whole testimony had dwindled down to, "I am going to go out and get two sticks and eat what I have left, and then my son and I are going to die." How is that for a compelling testimony?

The prophet Isaiah once said of the Lord, "A bruised reed shall he not break, and the smoking flax shall he not quench" (Isa. 42:3). This widow was a picture of a bruised reed, a candle that has almost gone out. God says, "I will not let go of those who know and love Me. I will not let their flame go out." The second half of that verse says, "He shall bring forth judgment unto truth." Here is the way I understand this verse: in the time of judgment, truth will become known again. The Lord is saying, "No, I will not let the fire of My people go out. Those who have only a spark left of seeking and knowing Me—even those who have been sitting in places where they should not have been sitting, listening to things they should not have been listening to—I will not let their flame go out. They are still part of My church, My bride, and I am going to reach out to them."

Here is the truth that will become known again in our generation:

Is not this the fast that I have chosen? to loose the bands of wickedness, to undo the heavy burdens, and to let the oppressed go free, and that ye break every yoke? Is it not to deal thy bread to the hungry [think of Elijah going to this widow], and that thou bring the poor that are cast out to thy house? when thou seest the naked, that thou cover him; and that thou hide not thyself from thine own flesh? (Isa. 58:6-7).

In the original text, to "hide not thyself from thine own flesh" means that we are not to hide from humankind. We are not to turn a blind eye to the pressing needs all around us, settling for a shallow Christianity with no power, no provision, no purpose and nothing to give. That kind of religion eventually becomes an obnoxious system of rules and regulations with nothing of God in it—a denial of the very reason Christ came to this earth.

Instead, I am confident that investing in people will once again become the hallmark of the true Church of Jesus Christ. Those who know God and are willing to obey Him will reach out to people who are losing heart. Although they will have to deal with their own hardship and may even end up with very little provision for themselves, God's people will once again allow the Lord to use their lives as an extension of His mercy.

As you and I make the choice to go to the widow and others in need in times of famine, not only will we be the hands that the Lord uses to sustain them, but this will bring life to us as well. We will actually sustain each other, for the Lord says that *this* will be our provision:

> And Elijah said unto her, Fear not; go and do as thou hast said: but make me thereof a little cake first, and bring it unto me, and after make for thee and for thy son. For thus saith the LORD God of Israel, The barrel of meal shall not waste, neither shall the cruse of oil fail, until the day that the LORD sendeth rain upon the earth. And she went and did according to the saying of Elijah: and she, and he, and her house, did eat many days. And the barrel of meal wasted not, neither did the cruse of oil fail, according to the word of the LORD, which he spake by Elijah (1 Kings 17:13-16).

When I first read this passage years ago, it seemed almost obnoxious to me that this man of God would come to the widow and demand that she provide for him before making a meal for herself and her son. At the time I did not recognize the greater principle embedded in this. The Lord was actually telling Elijah, "Teach her what I have taught you. Teach her to open her eyes to human need, to give to the hungry stranger, to give to others even out of the little that she has. As she does this, her supply will not fail. I will become her constant source of supply." *This* is how the kingdom of God works.

Simply put, if the day comes when all you have left is enough to make a peanut-butter sandwich, cut it in two and give half to the child across the hall who is going to school with no lunch. It isn't complicated; it never has been.

There was a time when I was pastoring in Canada, and an associate pastor came and told me that the motor in his car had just blown up. He sat across the desk from me and shook his head, saying, "I don't know what I am going to do. I don't have any savings. I don't know how I am going to buy groceries or even how I will take my family to church."

"Well, let's pray," I so kindly offered. So we bowed together, and I began to pray. All the while, I was well aware that I had $6,000 in the bank—my slush fund in case the ministry thing just didn't work out. That was roughly enough to buy a new Hyundai at that time.

As I began to pray, this voice in the back of my head said, "You hypocrite! Stop praying. You know very well that you have what this man needs." To be honest, I tried very hard to fight that thought. I attempted to keep praying, but it was as if my mouth was full of molasses that was getting thicker by the minute. The more I tried to pray, the more I just could not get the words out due to the abject hypocrisy. Here was my brother in Christ, a godly man who was in need, and I had exactly what would help him. In my mind I argued, "But, God, this money is all I have. What if I need it for my children? What about *my* car? It's not new—what if it breaks down too?"

Finally the Lord got a hold of me, and I went to the bank. I am telling you, the devil went to the bank with me—he was right over my shoulder the whole time! Nevertheless, I ended up withdrawing my savings, and I gave the funds to the associate pastor. I would like to be able to say that I left with joy after I put the money in his hand, but I didn't. I simply did it by faith and in obedience to what I knew the voice of God had said. It was soon after this that I left for eastern Canada and came back to find my house burned to the ground. So now I had lost my home, plus I had given my money away. As if that weren't enough, my car burned out too. By that point, I didn't have much left to say. Yet I chose to trust God.

A short time later I was up on a scaffold painting the dome of the old church we were restoring. Somebody came over and said to me, "Someone is calling you from the city—it's an emergency." I made my way down from the scaffold and went into my office to answer the phone. It turned out to be someone from a local car dealership, calling to tell me that a gentleman had come in that morning, bought a brand-new car and registered it in my name. "All you have to do is come in, sign for it and drive it away!" he said. I asked the name of the gentleman who had bought the car, but the salesman told me that the buyer wished to remain anonymous.

I believe that we are going to see miracles like this happening more frequently in the coming days. Now don't misunderstand me; I am not telling you that if you give somebody $6,000, you are going to get a new car. What I am telling you is that you do not have to fear investing in other people, even in your own time of need. God will supernaturally feed you. He will be your source and your strength.

We must settle this issue in our hearts now: Jesus Christ will be our provision. He will always be sufficient no matter what our need is, and He will always give us all that we need to accomplish what He calls us to do. Not only that, He will take the little bit that we have and multiply it—not merely for our own sake but for the sake of others.

Do you remember the miracle of the loaves—that familiar story when Jesus multiplied the five barley loaves and two fish and fed 5,000 men, plus women and children (see Mark 6:35-44)? Just as the disciples experienced, there will be moments when you look around and see nothing but a multitude of needs surrounding you. You may be tempted to conclude that you have little to give, but don't let that stop you from reaching out. Do not succumb to the thinking that God cannot do something through you, that your life is too insignificant to make any difference in this generation. The Lord is always willing to take you in your smallness and make you into more than you are. He delights in taking what little that you have and multiplying it in and through you that He alone might receive the glory. The day that a little boy gave five loaves and two fish, the Scriptures tell us that not only were the multitudes fed, but "they all ate as much as they wanted, and afterward, the disciples picked up twelve baskets of leftover bread and fish" (Mark 6:42-43, NLT).

This reminds me of another time when we were still living in Canada and about twenty people unexpectedly showed up at our house one Sunday. Included was a family with five children who had nowhere to go. Our finances were tight, and that day in particular all we had in the house was a pound of hamburger, some spaghetti noodles and two small cans of spaghetti sauce. Nevertheless, we invited everybody in. How do you turn away a hungry family?

Not knowing what else to do, my wife cooked what little we had, and then she began to ladle the spaghetti out. In her heart she felt God telling her, *Don't worry about it, just keep giving it out.* So that is exactly what she did—she simply kept dishing it out. In the end, twenty people were fed with that one pound of hamburger—it didn't run out! Not only that, we even had leftovers!

Despite the fact that it was a season in which we had to trust God to fill our own freezer, we also felt led to start a food bank, which eventually ended up feeding more than 200 families full time. The Lord never failed to supply for these families, nor did He fail to provide all that our family needed. One day a farmer showed up on our doorstep and told us the Lord had instructed him to fill our freezer with beef—and not just any beef but the meat of young cows, which is by far the most tender! He added, "As soon as your supply goes down, call me, and I will fill your freezer again."

This was the lesson in the miracle of the loaves. It was also what Elijah's camping by the brook had been all about: it was a season for God to teach Elijah that He is a God of the impossible. It was to prepare the prophet so that he could go to the widow and follow God's instructions, saying, "You give to God even out of the little that you have, and don't worry about the rest. He promises to keep us and sustain us."

TWELVE BASKETS ARE CALLING

One other significant lesson in the miracle of the loaves should be noted. Not only does this account convince us that God is a faithful provider of our needs and of the needs of those around us, it also stands as a reminder that investing in people will always be a choice—and not necessarily an easy one. It will often come at a personal cost, which we will see as we trace the journey of the disciples.

Immediately after the miraculous feeding of the 5,000, the Bible tells us that Jesus sent His disciples across the sea to Bethsaida. That evening a storm hit, and the disciples began to struggle against the fierce wind and waves. Suddenly Jesus came walking on the water toward them. As He got into the boat, to the disciples' amazement, the wind ceased, and they finally arrived in the land of Gennesaret (see Mark 6:45-53).

Now take a moment to picture the situation: The disciples have just been through an intense storm. They have been up rowing and toiling all night. They are no doubt tired and weary, and now they have landed in a strange place. Ahead of them are multitudes of people in need. Behind them are twelve baskets of leftover bread.

I see it almost as a test. Behind the disciples was a place of comfort—a place where there was provision for each of them. Up ahead was poverty, sickness and human need. To press forward meant that they would have to stay in their wet clothes and walk with Jesus toward those in need.

How easy it would have been at that point for the disciples to say, "What a rough trial we have been through! Thank God it is over now and we all made it through the storm! We know there are twelve baskets of bread left over back on the other side, and there are twelve of us disciples. Let's just row back across the sea." How easily they could have drafted their excuse and gone back to eat their bread. After all, they now had an incredible story to tell of how Jesus had brought them through their trial! They could have chosen to reverse their boat and concern themselves with their own safety and their own nourishment.

But that is not what the disciples did. Although they may still have had seaweed in their hair, they chose to move toward what Christ was doing. The Bible tells us that Jesus and His disciples stepped out of that boat and began to travel throughout the whole region—into villages, cities and the countryside. In other words, they entered into where the people were living—into people's pain, their sickness, their struggles, their religious confusion. They moved toward the people to meet them in their need. And the people ran about and began to carry in those who were sick and bring them to wherever Jesus was.

This scene once again provokes in my mind the obvious question: Shouldn't our seeking of God lead you and me toward human need? Shouldn't it cause us to get out of the boat of our own trials and tribulations in order to invest in other needy people, despite our own needs? We are all called to walk where Jesus walks, but we are still given a choice.

I mentioned Isaiah 58 earlier in this chapter as the mark of the true Church of Jesus Christ. It continues:

> If thou take away from the midst of thee the yoke, the putting forth of the finger, and speaking vanity; and if thou draw out thy soul to the hungry, and satisfy the afflicted soul; then shall thy light rise in obscurity, and thy darkness be as the noonday: and the LORD shall guide thee continually, and satisfy thy soul in drought, and make fat thy bones: and thou shalt be like a watered garden, and like a spring of water, whose

waters fail not. And they that shall be of thee shall build the old waste places: thou shalt raise up the foundations of many generations; and thou shalt be called, The repairer of the breach, The restorer of paths to dwell in (Isa. 58:9-12).

As we choose to reach out to human need, God promises that we will have light in our eyes even in the darkest hour. In the midst of confusion, we will have clarity of thought. Not only will the Lord continually keep and satisfy us, but something sovereign will also happen *through* us. The verse says that we shall be called "repairer of the breach." In other words, we will be used to begin to repair the breach that has allowed the enemy access to our society and our homes.

And so I implore you: go to the widow—that's what Elijah did. Move toward human need—that's what Jesus and His disciples did. Reach out to the impoverished and the oppressed and to those who have no helper; be a conduit of this incredible grace of God. You will discover that this will be your strength. This will be where God will manifest Himself as your provider, even in the days of famine ahead.

In all of this, may God give us wisdom. Reaching out to human need does not mean that you must empty your bank account and run out into the street and give it to the first person you see. However, it is time to be cognizant of the human need that surrounds us and to obey those inner promptings of the Holy Spirit. We must not turn a blind eye and close ourselves off by some river somewhere. Nor should we turn back to seek our own basket of bread, content to secure only our own provision. It is time that we have the courage to reach out to others rather than living the Christian life in order to accumulate as much as possible for ourselves. As we make the choice to invest in people, we will discover that the dividends will be paid not only in this life but for all eternity.

7

THE KEY TO
THE STOREHOUSE

*But whoso hath this world's good, and seeth his brother
have need, and shutteth up his bowels of compassion from him,
how dwelleth the love of God in him?*

1 JOHN 3:17

UNSHAKABLE

Our God is a God of infinite supply. The Scriptures tell us that the earth is His, and the fullness therein. The silver is His, the gold is His, as are the cattle on a thousand hills (see Ps. 24:1, 50:10; Hag. 2:8). Not only that, we also know that God is a good Father. Far surpassing the greatest earthly father, the Lord delights in providing for His children. So why then does it seem that we tap into so little of His endless supply?

As we have seen, choosing to invest in people is where it starts. However, we will soon discover that God has been working to produce something else in us all along—something essential for unlocking His endless supply. Even the most unlikely of heroes, once they found this key, were able to unlock incredible provision during a time of famine. We find their story in 2 Kings, and it begins with another season of intense hardship and famine:

> And it came to pass after this, that Benhadad king of Syria gathered all his host, and went up, and besieged Samaria. And there was a great famine in Samaria: and, behold, they besieged it, until an ass's head was sold for fourscore pieces of silver, and the fourth part of a cab of dove's dung for five pieces of silver (2 Kings 6:24).

This time the famine had hit Samaria, the northern part of Israel. Enemies had employed the classic tactic for conquering a city: surround it and starve the people out. Prices for even the most meager provisions had skyrocketed; things that literally held very little value were now absorbing the entirety of people's savings. Most of the food supply had been cut off, inciting a rush to get whatever was left. People resorted to previously unthinkable means, even cannibalism, in order to survive (see 2 Kings 6:28-29).

Whenever hardship strikes, who better to cast blame on than God and His servants? King Ahab accused Elijah of bringing trouble upon the nation when the rain had stopped. And now in this case, the king of Israel was so enraged by the suffering in Samaria that he concluded, "I am going to take Elisha's head off for this!" (see 2 Kings 6:31). In the same way, do not be surprised when we as followers of Christ become increasingly persecuted in the days to come.

Now the Lord had a message for the king of Israel, who by this point had become so weak that he was forced to lean upon his servant. Elisha said to him:

Hear ye the word of the LORD; Thus saith the LORD, To morrow about this time shall a measure of fine flour be sold for a shekel, and two measures of barley for a shekel, in the gate of Samaria. Then a lord on whose hand the king leaned answered the man of God, and said, Behold, if the LORD would make windows in heaven, might this thing be? (2 Kings 7:1-2).

God gave a word through Elisha that provision would very soon be made available and affordable, to which the servant of the king replied in disbelief, "Might this thing be?" In the *New Living Translation*, the servant says, "That couldn't happen even if the LORD opened the windows of heaven!"

You and I are living in a time when things can change drastically almost overnight. We New Yorkers recall how quickly the stores were emptied after the planes struck the Twin Towers on 9/11. If provisions were to suddenly become scarce again in the near future, we would do well to take to heart the psalmist's words: "I have been young, and now am old; yet have I not seen the righteous forsaken, nor his seed begging bread" (Ps. 37:25). Yet I wonder how many people will end up reacting to God's promise of provision with a sentiment of disbelief, much as the servant of the king of Israel did.

In response to the servant's remark, Elisha said, "You are going to see it with your eyes, but you will not partake of it" (see 2 Kings 7:2). What a stark reminder that we dare not deal casually with the Word of God—both the promises of God as well as the warnings of God. If this servant had possessed any wisdom in his heart, he would have said, "Oh God, forgive me for my unbelief! Forgive me for what I just said, for I know that You are faithful to keep Your Word." But sure enough, when the supply finally came into the city, this man was trampled by a stampede of people as they ran through the gate to get their hands on the provision.

THE MOST UNLIKELY OF PLANS

So what exactly was the plan of God in this scenario? What was the key to finally unlocking God's endless supply through the most unlikely of people?

> And there were four leprous men at the entering in of the gate: and they said one to another, Why sit we here until we die? If we say, We will enter into the city, then the famine is in the city, and we shall die there: and if we sit still here, we die

also. Now therefore come, and let us fall unto the host of the Syrians (2 Kings 7:3-4).

Four lepers! Keep in mind that this was not Plan B, this was Plan A. God had a king in the city, and there must have also been at least a minimal army left. Plus He had Elisha in the city, whose prayers had the power to literally blind opposing armies and bring them into captivity. There were a variety of plans that God could have employed. Yet with all these resources at hand, God chose to use four lepers in His incredible strategy to unleash provision. As these four headed toward the place where provision could be found, God struck terror into every force of hell that was starving the people. If there is such a thing as a volume button in heaven, the Lord put it to good use that day:

When they were come to the uttermost part of the camp of Syria, behold, there was no man there. For the Lord had made the host of the Syrians to hear a noise of chariots, and a noise of horses, even the noise of a great host: and they said one to another, Lo, the king of Israel hath hired against us the kings of the Hittites, and the kings of the Egyptians (vv. 5-7).

Although there were only four, God had finally found an "army" of people through whom He could unlock His supply. As these lepers headed down toward the Syrian camp, the Lord caused a thunderous sound to come to the very gates of hell itself. The enemy suddenly heard something that they knew they had no power to stand against, so they all fled.

Isn't it interesting how God chose the least likely of candidates to discover the place of His supply? If only you and I could lay hold of this truth and understand that victory is not by might, not by power, not by numbers, not by the eloquence of our preaching. In this case, victory was found when four struggling people, the weakest of society, simply headed toward a place where provision could be found. It was something that all the strategists in Samaria had overlooked. Nobody had considered this. Nobody had eyes to see what the plan of God really was. With the exception of Elisha and perhaps a few who were associated with him, faith, in great measure, was gone.

By the time the lepers arrived at the camp, they literally walked into an abundance of provision that had been completely abandoned—campfires were likely still burning, the soup still warm, horses and donkeys standing by, yet not a soul was there. Picture these four men reaching the uttermost part of the camp and pillaging the first tent they got to—eating and drinking to their hearts' content, then taking out the silver, gold and clothing and hiding it before setting off in search of more spoil. How exactly was God going to get glory from this? Why did He choose these lepers? I believe our answer is in the following verse:

> Then they said one to another, We do not well: this day is a day of good tidings, and we hold our peace: if we tarry till the morning light, some mischief will come upon us: now therefore come, that we may go and tell the king's household (2 Kings 7:9).

"We do not well!" In other words, "We have been basking in this provision. We understand that the enemy has been conquered, and now this incredible supply is here. But it is not just for us, it is for the people of the city. We do not well to hold our peace!"

God saw a core value in their character—something that must be in everyone before the true provision of God can be released through them—He saw compassion. And because of the heart He saw within these men, He sent them out as the virtual key to unlocking a storehouse of supply for the nation.

The word "compassion" means "sympathy, pity, an inner moving or yearning that moves one to doing something about the situation." Unfortunately, sometimes compassion fails to be the undergirding reason why people move toward the mountains of human need. Instead, our motive may be to prove a theological point or even an inner obligation to prove the existence of God to ourselves if not to anybody else. Other times it may be an attempt to earn favor with God. Then there are those who attend churches that make them feel obligated to become involved in their social programs.

I don't know about you, but I would rather be filled with the compassion of God. I would rather give because my heart is stirred by the Holy Spirit to help those who are in need. I would rather move in the compassion of Christ instead of the compulsion of religion. There is a difference.

I thank God that it was not out of obligation but rather out of compassion that Jesus gave His life for you and me. I am grateful that the cross was not just some legal proving ground for Him to say, "I am going to do My part—now you must do yours." No, it was the absolute compassion of Jesus that caused His arms to be nailed wide open to "whosoever will come" and receive the supply of His life. The provision of Christ's life was opened to us through a compassionate Savior, and it will always be open to the world through a Church that has embraced His heart of compassion for its generation.

Keep in mind that compassion does not mean sorrow, as is the common misunderstanding. If I become a compassionate person, it does not mean that I walk down the street, constantly hanging my head in sorrow over all the human need around me. No, compassion goes much deeper than sorrow. It is an inner moving of the heart, born of God, that compels us to cry, "Lord, You must release through my hands whatever is needed in this situation. It is not right that Your creation should be in such a state. It is not right that Your children should be hungry, that the house of God should be in bondage, that somebody should not know the freedom that Christ has fully purchased for them on Calvary. God Almighty, release it through my hands!"

This kind of cry was in the heart of the four lepers. They were aware of a starving society out there, and their compassion would not allow them to simply dismiss the predicament of others—no matter *who* those people were.

THE CHOICE TO FORGIVE

This brings us to a significant point in the story of the lepers. It is one thing to invest in people who have never hurt us. The widow who Elijah went to never did him any harm. Likewise, the disciples had never even encountered the people across the sea at Gennesaret before they landed there. However, it is another thing to be moved with compassion toward people who have wronged us. In the case of the four lepers, think about how tempting it would have been for them to neglect, and thus get vengeance on, a city that had subjected them to incredible pain and rejection.

It is important to understand how lepers were treated in those days. Whenever lepers were actually allowed inside the city, they were required to cover their faces and cry out, "Unclean! Unclean!" Everywhere they walked, people would flee from them. Notice as well that the lepers had initially concluded, "If we stay here, we are going to starve." That means they were outside the gate—the absolute last in the city to be fed. The pecking order in that society would have been the king first, followed by his soldiers, and then the families. In other words, priority would go to those of greatest influence or wealth in society, leaving lepers at the very bottom of the totem pole.

When the four of them arrived at the camp, they could easily have said, "Let all the other people suffer and starve, just as we did. We have found all the provision we need. Let the rest of the city figure out how to get out of this mess on their own!" Perhaps today you find a similar sentiment deep within your heart. You may have moved to a new city hoping to find opportunities around every corner, only to realize that things are not unfolding quite the way you envisioned. You thought a measure of kindness would be extended to you, but you instead found yourself being pushed to the side as everyone else passes you by. As a Christian in this last hour, you are going to discover incredible provision from heaven. You must be careful, however, lest the thought enter your heart, *This is for me and me alone. I am going to eat my morsel by myself, here in my little corner of security. When this all blows over, I am going to emerge as the one whom God provided for. Who cares about my neighbors? What have they ever done for me?*

Thankfully that was not the reaction of the four lepers. I am not sure that the king would have acted as righteously as they did. I am not sure that some of the other people would not have taken the resources for themselves. Living as lepers had somehow worked something into their hearts. Perhaps it was an understanding of what it was like to live a life of rejection, suffering and pain. In any event, these men were moved with compassion, and consequently they exemplified the heart of

Christ. As we see in their situation, this will often require that we walk in forgiveness. We must be willing to go back into a city that has caused us pain, willing to go back to neighbors or co-workers who were unkind to us.

WHEN THE BETRAYERS SHOW UP

Even Joseph had to choose to forgive his brothers when he found himself with access to the provision they needed. Sometimes in life when we have been deeply hurt, we tend to draw back and become cautious with people, determined not to allow them to wound us again. I am sure that must have been in Joseph's heart at least in some measure, for before the years of famine came, he named his firstborn son Manasseh, which means "God has made me to forget all my hardship and all my father's house" and his second son Ephraim, for he said, "God has caused me to be fruitful in the land of my affliction" (see Gen. 41:51-52). It was as if he had moved past the pain of it all and was rejoicing in the fulfillment of God's promise to him . . . until suddenly before him in physical form was the memory of a very deep betrayal. There stood his starving brothers in front of him, hat in hand. Joseph knew that he had God's provision to feed them, and so he was faced with a choice.

We would like to think Joseph just ran to his brothers with open arms in the same way the father of the Prodigal Son did. However, I believe there was a tremendous struggle in that man's heart. The Bible tells us that Joseph sought a secret place and wept. Don't you think it was incredibly difficult for him at that moment? Can you imagine the memories of thirteen years of anguish—suffering, hardship, imprisonment and betrayal—suddenly welling up within him? When he finally made himself known to his brethren, the Scripture says that he wailed so loudly that the whole house of Pharaoh heard him (see Gen. 45:2).

Sometimes there will be pain involved in the choices that we must make. Yet just as the four lepers had done, Joseph chose to forgive those who had hurt him and allowed himself to be moved with the compassion of God for them. That is why God unlocked a supply through his hands. During Joseph's journey, God needed to bring very undesirable circumstances into his life in order to open his spiritual eyes; to work into his heart a compassion that would allow him to forgive his family; to give him hands to unlock a storehouse. When Joseph forgave and embraced his brothers, provision was opened to his entire family, and they continued to prosper for generations to come.

IN THE BELLY OF THE SHIP

Paul faced a similar choice when he found himself in the midst of the storm. He was most likely chained in the bottom of the ship, as was the common practice for transporting prisoners. When he warned the people not to undertake this journey, he was scoffed at and scorned—much like those who speak for Christ today. The voice of truth is constantly marginalized and set aside as irrelevant, bigoted and out of touch. Eventually it is locked away in the same way that Paul was relegated to the bottom of the ship.

Imagine the unspeakable hardship that Paul once again faced. He was probably surrounded by disgruntled prisoners who ranted and cursed all the more as the storm intensified. Polluted waters would have filled the bottom of the ship as it was tossed about, the scent of death adding to the dreadful atmosphere. Throughout the ordeal, Paul knew that he was being carried on this journey by the spiritual ignorance of those who had refused to heed the word of God. In the same way, you may find yourself in a dark and stormy place, and you can readily point to somebody somewhere who was the source of your pain—who caused you to be on a journey that you would not normally have been on.

Nevertheless, in the midst of it all, Paul chose in his heart to forgive these men and pray, "God, would You be merciful to those who have afflicted me? Would You be merciful to those who have put me in chains and caused me such pain? Would You be merciful to the captain of the ship, who scoffed at my word of warning and instead sent me down to the belly of hell? And when this whole thing falls apart, would You give me a word of life for these people?"

Isn't that amazing? Paul, once an intolerant Pharisee who hauled people out of their homes and tortured them to get them to blaspheme the name of Christ, was now moved with compassion for his oppressors! The opposition he faced along his journey had worked in him the ability to be kind, even to those who least deserved it.

COMPASSION TO MEET THE DEPTH OF DEPRAVITY

Unlike the case with Joseph and Paul, you may sometimes discover that it is not necessarily people who have done you personal harm that you must forgive. A day is soon approaching when society will reach such a depth of depravity that loving people at all will become increasingly difficult. There will be days when our flesh will argue, "But Lord, have You seen the way people are? Have You seen what they are doing to Your name? Have You seen how they are breaking down everything I hold dear, destroying the very fabric of our society? Have You heard their rants and ravings? I would rather have You judge them than love them through me!"

The Lord would say to you and to me in reply, "Oh, yes, I see what they are doing. But have you forgotten that one day I was on a cross? One day people like these were walking by Me, wagging their heads and taunting, 'He says He is the Son of God. Let His Father save Him! He saved others, but He cannot save Himself. Come down from the cross, and we will believe You!'" Think about it for a moment. When Jesus spoke those words on the cross, "Father, forgive them, for they know not what they do," the soldiers were at the foot of the cross, casting lots for His clothing! What an astounding picture of divine love against human depravity!

Paul said it this way: "I will very gladly spend and be spent for you; though the more abundantly I love you, the less I be loved" (2 Cor. 12:15). I believe this is exactly where we are headed. The more abundantly we love, the more compassionately we reach out, the less it will be reciprocated in the coming days. When kind words and gestures are met with indifference or scorn, we all naturally tend to withdraw our hands, turn away from the rejection and call for judgment. There is something within us that says, "Enough! I don't have to deal with this." However, we have no excuse for becoming like-spirited with the people of this world.

The bottom line is that we must have the compassion of God flowing out through us. How do we get to such a place? Not merely by study. We might wish we could take a Bible course somewhere and come out compassionate, but it just doesn't work that way. Compassion comes by allowing the One who already won the battle for kindness to do His work in and through us. All the trials we are going through are working to produce something in our hearts that will bring us to a place where our hands are freely open to all people, despite their response. It does not matter whether people appreciate it or not, whether they are honest or dishonest. Remember, God's hands are open, and He sends rain on the just and the unjust.

I am well aware that I cannot forgive or love with that kind of divine love, and neither can you. Human effort cannot produce the kind of compassion required to reach a perishing world or the kind of forgiveness that the greatest depths of depravity demand. It is supernatural and must be worked in us by God. Try as you might to love people in your own strength, you will find that words of grace and forgiveness will not be in your mouth unless they are supernaturally put there by Almighty God. Learning to love the unlovely requires a change of heart and a molding of character. Something of God must be worked into your life by the Holy Spirit, and most often this is accomplished during times of trial.

SUFFERING BEGETS KINDNESS

Every Sunday morning, I walk across the platform in our sanctuary and pray for an hour before service. People coming into the church who see me pacing back and forth might conclude, *Oh, what a man of faith! He is probably moving mountains with his prayers right now.* But I will tell you honestly that some weeks as I have paced back and forth, my prayer has been more along the lines of, "God, I can't do this. I don't know how to win this victory!" And my concerns are not even necessarily about the service or what I am going to preach. They are regarding issues and situations in my own heart and my own life. *I don't know how to get through the imprisonment, the abandonment, the betrayal.*

When I come out on the other side of each trial, however, something is formed within me. I emerge from the fire wondering, *Where did this fruit in my life come from?* I notice things in my heart that were not in me before I went into the trials. There is a compassion that I did not possess before. There is an ability to forgive that I know is supernatural.

The strange thing about the kingdom of God is that suffering begets kindness. It does not make sense to the natural mind. I do not completely understand how the trials work to produce God's compassion in our hearts. I just know that it works. Somehow we emerge from trials with kindness, not wanting anyone else to be wounded. Suddenly our hearts and hands are open to all people.

God must have a people who possess tender hands and compassionate hearts in this generation. Compassion is the embodiment of the heart of God, and therefore this ought to be the essence of the heart of His Church. If we ever lose the compassion of Christ, we lose everything, including the keys to the true provision of God in our generation. Without His compassion, all we will do when the famine hits is condemn everybody around us. We will point fingers and seek vengeance on those who have wronged us rather than represent Christ to a generation that very soon is going to need the tender hand of God. Yet if we are willing to move with compassion wherever God calls us, we will be amazed at the resources He will multiply through our hands—along with an endless supply of joy.

8

THE LAST BANK
IN AMERICA

For, behold, the darkness shall cover the earth, and gross
darkness the people: but the LORD shall arise upon thee,
and his glory shall be seen upon thee. And the Gentiles shall
come to thy light, and kings to the brightness of thy rising.
Lift up thine eyes round about, and see:
all they gather themselves together, they come to thee.

ISAIAH 60:2-4

UNSHAKABLE

S hortly before Jesus went to the cross, His disciples had a question for Him: what will be the sign of Your coming? Jesus proceeded to describe the perilous times that would come upon the world before His soon return, which then led to another question. This time it was Jesus who posed the question:

> Who then is a faithful and wise servant, whom his lord hath made ruler over his household, to give them meat in due season? Blessed is that servant, whom his lord when he cometh shall find so doing. Verily I say unto you, That he shall make him ruler over all his goods (Matt. 24:45-47).

Who then is a faithful and wise servant? When the darkness sets in, there will be servants who will be no different from the fearful in the world. Everything that they trusted in will be dead and gone, and their eyes will be fixed solely on the destruction and hopelessness all around. On the other hand, there will be servants whose treasure was not found in this world but rather in Christ. These will be the faithful and wise servants who will have something of substance to offer those around them. In other words, they will be the ones who make up the true Church of Jesus Christ, rising up to fulfill her call and purpose on this earth. What a glorious sight it will be!

This is why we need not fear what is to come. You see, no matter how harrowing the days ahead, I believe we are on the verge of a spiritual awakening in America. What is the evidence of an awakening? It begins when you and I once again become one with the heart of God, understanding what it truly means to declare ourselves to be followers of Christ. It is when we make the choice to move away from our own dreams—our own image of what our life and future should be—and set our eyes on eternity and on the souls around us. That is when God begins to stir us, and our ears become open to a cry being raised in our midst.

I can already hear that deep cry sounding all around us in this generation. Many people are starting to sink in despair. All of this marks the beginning of what I feel we have set before us—a short window of time when people will want to hear from God again. It is in times of crisis that people are finally ready to listen. The widow was willing to listen to Elijah's instructions. Those on the sinking ship were ready to hear what Paul had to say.

In the previous chapter, we left Paul in the belly of the ship, having made the choice to forgive those around him. Suddenly, in the midst of his difficulty, a window opened. I can picture a simple message coming to Paul, "The captain has sent for you."

By that point, the ship was already going down, panic had set in, and the captain must have concluded, "We have run out of ideas; everything is falling apart. Where is that man who told us that we shouldn't go on this journey? I want to hear what he has to say!" All of a sudden, out of the belly of hell, out of circumstances that would have overwhelmed an ordinary man without the Spirit of God within, emerged this man Paul.

Standing on that deck, Paul's life was a compelling testimony of the keeping power of God. He had been at the bottom of the ship praying, and he had found victory—not *from* his situation but rather *in* his situation. Paul's circumstances did not necessarily change, for when he was brought up on deck, he was still a captive. He was still in chains, still being led on his journey to stand before Caesar. Nevertheless, he stood in absolute victory! He clearly possessed an inner strength that was supernatural, and he was filled with the absolute joy of being surrendered to Jesus Christ. Paul had reached a place of being fully given for others, despite his own pain and hardship. The love of God for souls was what propelled this man, and now he was prepared with a word for the season in which he and his companions found themselves.

The Lord gave Paul a word of exhortation for the people—a message of mercy, not of condemnation. He started by essentially saying, "You should have listened, but you didn't. But now I am telling you that I have been in the presence of God, and He is a merciful God. He has told me that He is going to spare all of your lives." How clearly Paul fulfilled the Scripture as that faithful and wise servant, giving others meat in due season! After he exhorted them with those words of hope, Paul even urged all of them to take some meat.

What happened next is astounding. With massive waves crashing all around them and threatening to overturn the ship, the sails in tatters, a seasick and terrified crew—Paul took bread, gave thanks and broke it before everyone, right there on the deck of the ship! In other words, Paul held one of the most profound communion services in the entire New Testament other than the Last Supper. In the end, although the ship was destroyed, all 276 lives were spared for a season. It was a mercy call, and these people were given another chance to hear about the salvation of God in Christ Jesus.

FOR THE SAKE OF OTHERS

In the coming days, the fearful will be searching for answers. Those who have lost all sense of security will be trying to find something of true value to hold onto. People who have been disappointed in the church will be looking for the real Jesus. They will be gripped with sorrow, desperate for a word of encouragement.

It is the mercy of God that will cause people to come running to the true followers of Christ. You will find that those who previously disregarded you will suddenly be interested in everything that God has put in your heart, just as those on the ship were with Paul. In the midst of that storm, the captain and crew must have stood there in amazement and wondered, "What makes this man so confident? He is in the same predicament we are in, yet he seems to be so full of hope! Why does he see a future when we see destruction? What is inside this man that makes him different from us?" Likewise, people will suddenly start coming to you, asking why you have such hope. Even those who once mocked and ridiculed you are going to wonder what is different about you. As the apostle Peter said, we must be ready to give an answer to those who ask the reason for the hope that is in us (see 1 Pet. 3:15).

Note that these people will not be looking for some new theory on God. Our generation does not need another Bible study, nor do they need people who merely present a series of facts and figures about God to them. It is not sufficient to throw a tract on somebody's desk and hope it will make a difference, as good as that may be. No! People need encouragement from someone who has endured suffering and has come to know God in the midst of it. They need to hear from somebody who has the reality of an experience with the Lord; somebody whose life is yielded to God and therefore is empowered by Him.

As these people come your way, you will finally understand why you have been through all the trials and opposition; why you seemingly had it so hard when it appeared that everyone else had it so easy. Finally you will have a real and personal revelation that it has all been for the sake of other people. Consider the words that Paul wrote to the Philippian church:

> For to me, to live is Christ, and to die is gain. But if I live on in the flesh, this will mean fruit from my labor; yet what I shall choose I cannot tell. For I am hard-pressed between the two, having a desire to depart and be with Christ, which is far better. Nevertheless to remain in the flesh is more needful for you. And being confident of this, I know that I shall remain and continue with you all for your progress and joy of faith (Phil. 1:21-25, *NKJV*).

Paul was saying, "I have this confidence that the Lord is leaving me where I presently am, and will possibly leave me here tomorrow, for you." Amazing! "He is bringing me through the valley of the shadow of death not just for my sake but for yours!"

By the time his brothers showed up in Egypt, Joseph had reached the same understanding. As he finally revealed his identity to them, he gave them this reassurance: "Don't be upset, and don't be angry with yourselves for selling me to this place. It was God who sent me here ahead of you to preserve your lives. . . . God has sent me ahead of you to keep you and your families alive and to preserve many survivors" (Gen. 45:5,7, NLT). Joseph finally understood that God had precisely appointed all the trials he had endured over the years. They were all for a specific purpose—for the sake of his family and many others!

This, in great measure, is what it means when the Scriptures exhort us to offer our lives as a living sacrifice, which is our reasonable service (see Rom. 12:1). It is the willingness to be brought through our present trials instead of looking for a quick way out, understanding that it may be necessary for God to leave us in difficult places for the sake of others.

How foreign a concept to this present generation that Jesus would allow us to suffer for somebody else's sake! This does not make sense if our whole focus of being a Christian is all about ourselves. But once we understand that the Church is left on the earth for the sake of others, then the suffering and trials we have to go through start to make sense. You finally realize that you are somebody's Joseph; you are somebody's Paul. You are the exact prescription of God for somebody who will be coming to you for help and for hope.

HE IS CALLING YOU!

Just as Pharaoh sent for Joseph and loosed him, and just as the captain called Paul to the deck of the ship, one day when the King of kings needs you, He is going to call for you. Not some superstar, not some high profile preacher somewhere—you! Suddenly you will find yourself with keys to a supply of God in your hand.

God will call for you because you recognized the purpose of suffering in the Christian life and did not resist the work that He was doing in you. You allowed the Lord to take you through the floods, famines, storms and trials—trusting that He had a divine purpose. He was preparing you to have tender hands and a receiving heart, forming within you compassion to open the doorway to everlasting life in Christ. Through it all you learned something about the keeping power of Christ that could come no other way but through the fire.

And now as you are committed to the work of God on the earth—choosing to invest in people, even those who are difficult to love—the Lord is placing something in your hand. He is unlocking His provision *to* you as well as *through* you. He is giving you an authority and a strength that is supernatural. As you continually reach out to others, everything that was purchased on Calvary will flow through your hands. Just like Paul, you will have the ability to speak to people as an encourager. You will be able to lift them out of darkness, to speak against what oppresses their minds and to watch as strongholds begin to dissolve.

How you will count it all worthwhile when you realize that everything God allowed in your life was purposed to bring you to a place where one day it is nothing but Jesus! Nothing but His will is yours, nothing but His voice is your voice—it will be nothing of yourself but all of Him. Jesus will be your only hope and strength. The mercy of God is bringing you to a place where your message will be all about Him—the complete sufficiency of Jesus Christ. It is in that place that you will remain unshakable, no matter what comes.

In a spiritually bankrupt age, you will be God's stimulus package to stir up society everywhere you go, simply by letting God be God in you and allowing your heart to be drawn to people. There will soon be no other bank people can go to; no other ATM, no other deposit, no other institution that can be trusted. But there will always be a testimony for Jesus Christ. There will always be a Church where people can go and withdraw something of lasting value. There will be a people inside of whom God has put the deposit of His Holy Spirit. No strategies, no seven steps—nothing but Jesus.

God will always have a living testimony in the earth—a testimony that He carries His people through every trial. And I am confident that you will be among those who hold forth the Word of life—not merely speaking about God's keeping power but rather being a visible demonstration. Something of God will be birthed deep within your heart: a refined faith in His faithfulness. It will be the pure gold of confident faith in a God who has not only spoken to you but who lives within you.

In the coming days, when all else begins to fail, you will offer more hope than any theory, philosophy or bailout package that could ever be proposed. As people continually come your way, you will soon discover that the "last bank in America" is you! Always open. And the supply is endless.

TIMES SQUARE ■ CHURCH

Visit Times Square Church at:

1657 Broadway
New York, New York 10019

(212) 541-6300

www.tscnyc.org

YOU CAN BE FREE
FROM FEAR

Uncertainty is a feature of the modern world, from widespread unemployment and financial insecurity to wars and rumors of wars. It's impossible to know from one day to the next what will happen. Yet in an hour when fear is mounting on every side, God desires you to live free from fear. In *Fear Not*, pastor Carter Conlon shows you how to receive a new spirit in place of uncertainty and fearfulness—a spirit of power and love. You will discover how to claim this spirit by choosing to follow Christ, giving you the power to face life's most difficult challenges, and see that God's love casts out every fear!

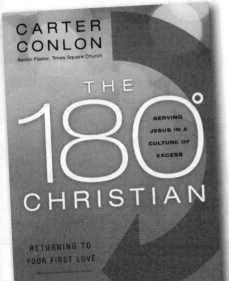

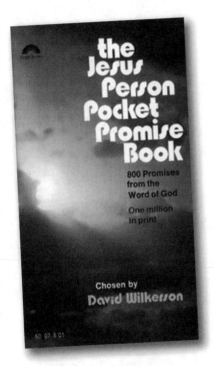

MORE TITLES BY
CARTER CONLON

Quiet Times
Music CD

**Where Christmas
Never Ends**
Music CD

Day by Day
Music CD

**Clunky of
Maryborough**
Children's Book

**Katie & the Dogs
Are Gone!**
Children's Book

**Every Good House
Needs a Mouse**
Children's Book

Petey Yikes!
Children's Book

Buy a Book, Feed a Child!

100% of the net proceeds from the sale of these children's books will benefit ChildCry, a ministry of Times Square Church (NYC) that feeds hungry children throughout the world. For more information visit: **childcrynyc.org**

To purchase or learn more about these titles visit our web store at: **tscnyc.org**